# Guerra Fantástica

## The Portuguese Army and the Seven Years War

**António Barrento**

Foreword by Charles Esdaile

Helion & Company

Helion & Company Limited
Unit 8 Amherst Business Centre
Budbrooke Road
Warwick
CV34 5WE
England
Tel. 01926 499619
Email: info@helion.co.uk
Website: www.helion.co.uk
Twitter: @helionbooks
blog.helion.co.uk/

Published by Helion & Company 2020
Designed and typeset by Mach 3 Solutions Ltd (www.mach3solutions.co.uk)
Cover designed by Paul Hewitt, Battlefield Design (www.battlefield-design.co.uk)

 Originally published as *Guerra Fantástica 1762. Portugal, o Conde de Lippe e a Guerra does Sete Anos* (Lisbon: Tribuna da História, 2006). This English translation includes a new foreword and some updates to the text.

Cover: Background – details from 'The Capture of Almeida' (Drawing attributed to Cavaleiro Faria in *Notícias dos Sucessos da Guerra de Hespania*, belonging to the Library of the Military Academy, Lisbon, doc. 2058) and 'Siege of Almeida, a city of Portugal in the Province of Trás-os-Montes [sic], by the Spanish, upon orders of General Marquis of Sarria, from 11 to 25 August 1762' (Engraving by Lieutenant Engineer L. Therbu and engraved by Henro Contgen, engraver at the Court and the University of Mainz). Figures – soldier from the Infantry Regiment of Porto; officer from the Companhias de Éguas of Beira (Mapa do Fardamento que por ordem de S. Mag, Se fes na Cidade do Porto debaixo da inspecção do Tenente Gn.al João de Almada, Military Historical Archives, Lisbon).



ISBN 978-1-911628-11-8

British Library Cataloguing-in-Publication Data.
A catalogue record for this book is available from the British Library.

# Contents

# Acknowledgements

I wish to express my gratitude to Lieutenant-General Ferreira dos Santos, Commander of the Military Academy, and Colonel Marçal Lourenço, Director of the Library of this institution, for allowing access to the manuscript of the Military Academy that has been frequently used to illustrate this work and from which the main image of the cover of this book was taken; to Colonel Ribeiro de Faria, Director of the Military Museum, for providing me with the images of the two portraits of the Count of Lippe used in this book, and to Rui Fonseca, for making available the Plan of the siege of the Fortress of Almeida.

# Foreword

As any student of the Peninsular War is aware, the border between Spain and Portugal is studded with fortresses that played a key role in the campaigns of the Duke of Wellington and his opponents, pride of place amongst these strongholds going to Elvas and Badajoz in the south and Almeida and Ciudad Rodrigo in the south. That said, what they are less likely to be aware of is the long history of hostility that gave birth to them. Dating from the Middle Ages, this hostility led to repeated clashes in the course of the eighteenth century, it therefore being fair to say that the Spaniards and Portuguese were as unnatural bed-fellows as the Spaniards and the British. In itself this constitutes an interesting perspective on the struggle of 1808-14, but what is still more the case is the fact that the last of these clashes – the brief campaign of 1761-1762 – in many ways prefigured the 1810 invasion of Portugal by the army of Marshal Masséna. Indeed, in some ways it was even more dramatic: whereas the 'darling child of victory' more-or-less succeeded in keeping his starving men together, in 1761-1762 his French and Spanish predecessors were reduced to a state of utter ruin.

What we have, then, is an event of considerable significance which on the one hand provided Wellington with the inspiration for his defence of Portugal in 1810-1811 – the scorched-earth tactics, construction of impregnable field fortification, and integration of 'little war' with conventional military operations were all just as much on show in 1761-1762 as they were some 50 years later and on the other should have suggested to Napoleon that the conquest of Portugal by Masséna or anyone else was out of the question. As the events of the *Guerra Fantastica* were well known in France, it is at first sight difficult to see why so avid a student of history as the emperor should not immediately have grasped their significance. The answer lies in part, of course, in the French ruler's increasingly shaky grasp of strategic realities, but, as the author of this Foreword has argued elsewhere, just as important was the fact that the chief French historian of the campaign, Dumouriez, the victor of Valmy, had painted a picture in which the blame for the disaster lay in part with the perceived uselessness of the Spaniards and in part with the fact that the invasion had been led by cautious generals of the *ancien régime* who had little idea how to wage war. Whereas Wellington was deeply impressed with the repulse of the Franco-Spanish armies and sought to apply its lessons to the threats which he confronted, Napoleon therefore wrote off the episode and dispatched Masséna upon a fool's errand. All this being the case, I commend this work to the attention of all those interested in the Peninsular War just as much as I do to all those interested in the campaigns of a half-century hitherto.

Charles J. Esdaile,
University of Liverpool

1

# The Concept of a 'Fantastical War'

In 1762 Portugal became involved in what would later be called the Seven Years War. The Portuguese of this period used the expression *Guerra Fantástica* – Fantastical War – to refer to the part of the conflict that occurred in Portuguese territory. It was fantastical because nobody thought that it would develop the way it did. It seemed more a figment of the imagination than a product of reality. People were surprised not only by what happened, but also by what did not happen.

It was fantastical because this conflict was devoid of any of the battles or clashes between armies that usually occur between belligerent armies in a war and often determine the winners and losers. In fact, what occurred in this case was, rather than a frontal clash between two armies, a 'warlike war' (*guerra guerreada*), that is, a war through incursions, in the sense in which medieval chronicler Fernão Lopes used this expression while writing about the debate that had been held in 1385 on how to defend the kingdom from neighbouring Castille.

It was fantastical because it was perceived by the Portuguese, save for a few more enlightened individuals who viewed it as a means of counteracting the unacceptable positions of Spain and France, as cataclysmic in character (a sort of extension of the earthquake of 1755, which was still a fresh memory, having only occurred seven years before). In fact, the war would bring a trail of death and destruction to the kingdom. Yet, while death and destruction occurred, reality did not amount either to what had been dreaded or to what might have been expected considering the inequality of the forces on both sides.

It was fantastical because neither the objectives that the enemy intended to achieve nor the manoeuvres that its army carried out are well understood, in contrast to the clear Portuguese aim of defence of the kingdom. Moreover, it was fantastical because the war happened from a distance, in the region of the border with Spain, never reaching the coast or even the central part of the country.

It was fantastical because, apart from a few clashes and the fall of some forts, what happened was a succession of marches and counter-marches, which amounted to a permanent game aimed at limiting the freedom of action and the superiority of the enemy. Furthermore, it was fantastical because an incapable army, as was the Portuguese army on the eve of the invasion, was transformed into a force of some value in a very short period of time. It was thus a fantastical war in which the defence of the kingdom was achieved against forces that were much superior to its own.

Finally, it was fantastical because, despite Portugal's reduced power as compared with that of Spain and France, which stood together in a coalition, Portugal managed to use diplomacy in a skilful way, to gain the support of the allies, to improve the quality of its military force and prevent the enemy from achieving its intended goals.

Yet, while this war could seem fantastical to most of the Portuguese then, it appears more natural now when viewed upon an analysis of the developments that took place in Europe in the previous years and the circumstances in which it occurred. Taking this into consideration, before proceeding into narrating the military campaign of 1762, this work will first consider its general evolution, as well as some events that make it easier to understand this conflict, how Portugal became involved in it, and the manner in which military operations took place.

2

# The Environment in Europe

The environment in Europe during the period that led up to the Seven Years War (1756-1763) was characterised by developments in the domains of society, politics, economics and knowledge, which largely explain the tensions that existed, the conflicts that took place and the war that flared up.

While many aspects were influential with respect to this war, some were particularly relevant. In order to understand the reasons for this conflict, it is necessary, much as in other situations, to look into conjunctural elements of change. In the case of this war, one must bear in mind the evolution that had been occurring in politics and society, the progress of science and technology, European expansion and colonisation, and the importance of the economy and trade. A brief consideration of these factors makes it easier to understand the small period of about one year during which Portugal was involved in the Seven Years War.

## Politics and Society

In terms of ideas, political institutions and society, fundamental changes took place during the transition to the second half of the second millennium that followed the arrival of Vasco da Gama in India. This was a period of constant collapse of feudalism, a form of societal living that had existed in Europe for hundreds of years (since the 'barbarians' had settled in the decaying Roman Empire), and of gradual centralisation of royal power. Society was still made up of three orders, following a hierarchical form of social organisation that had been developing throughout the Middle Ages. The clergy, in both its secular and regular branches, had the mission of leading man to eternal life or salvation. It was the responsibility of the nobility to guarantee the safety of all. The people had the duty of obtaining the goods that everybody needed. The price to be paid for the advantages derived from the 'specialisation' of duties was that of celibacy and detachment from material goods for the clergy, that of potential blood tribute for the nobility, and that of constant labour or work for the people.[1]

1 André Corvisier, *História Universal - O Mundo Moderno* (Lisboa: Círculo dos Leitores, 1977), p.84.

Magnet block probably offered by the Emperor of China to João V. It was later mounted by the Englishman William Dugood, who was a member of the Royal Society of London, on this table. It may have been meant for the Experimental Physics Unit of the Oratorian priests, who were based at the Convent of the Congregation in Lisbon, which later became the Palácio das Necessidades. It belonged to the collection of the College of Noblemen, founded in 1761, and in 1772 it was transferred to the Experimental Physics Unit of Coimbra. (Museum of Physics of the University of Coimbra).

While this segmentation of society continued to exist during the two centuries that preceded the Seven Years War, the bourgeoisie was to become ever more important as a result of its ability to take the initiative in various fields, the gradual increase of its economic power, and its desire for social upward mobility. Its ability to take the initiative and its growing economic power are found in its pursuit of trade on a more intensive and global scale. A new pattern of trade now emerged in the setting up of fairs that were larger in terms both of space and traded commodities, in the exploitation and development of necessary and profitable activities, and in the purchase of property that the nobility could not afford to maintain. Social mobility is the result from a natural desire of human beings to achieve well-being and to gain respect and prestige. This situation was well caricatured in *Auto do Fidalgo Aprendiz* by Francisco Manuel de Mello and *Le Bourgeois-Gentilhomme* by Molière. Simultaneously, the nobles of the sword, or knights, were facing a situation of decline that was fully portrayed in *Don Quixote* by Cervantes.

As royal power became supreme by means of the gradual erasure of the influence of the nobility, monarchs throughout most of Continental Europe endorsed and subscribed to the political thought of major supporters of centralised power, such as Machiavelli with the precocious political treatise *The Prince* (1513), Bodin with *The Six Books of the Republic* (1576), Thomas Hobbes with *Leviathan* (1641) and Bossuet with *Politics Drawn from the Very Words of Holy Scripture* (1709). On the whole, they upheld the figure of the 'Prince' as the exclusive holder of power, as an entity that was both entitled and duty-bound to manage tensions between men within each political society, to respect and preserve the natural law, and to respond to internal and external threats. This was a movement of near sacralisation of power and the monarch.

While Machiavelli was apologetic of pragmatism and the supremacy of politics over morality, Bossuet, who was the tutor of the Dauphin, viewed royal authority as a form of the power of God as transmitted to men; the connection of the king with his people was therefore the embodiment of the paternal character of the monarchy.[2] It is against the background of the circulation of these political ideas that Louis XIV, during whose reign absolute monarchy reached its highest form in France, stated in his memoirs

2 J. Jacques Chevalier, *Les Grandes Oeuvres Politiques de Machiavel à Nos Jours* (Paris: Colin, 1970), p.73.

that 'if the name of lord belongs to us by right of birth, the name of father must be the sweetest object of our ambition'.[3]

In contrast with the solid establishment of absolute monarchy that occurred throughout Continental Europe by means of the slow gradual dismissal of the courts and assemblies, in England the Parliament acquired an ever greater importance from the seventeenth century (even obtaining complete power for a time in the aftermath of the Civil Wars), which resulted in limitations in various matters to the power of the sovereign, even though he was, since Henry VIII, the head of the Anglican Church.

In the same way that absolute monarchy was sustained by the authors and the works mentioned above, the regime obtained ideological support from a number of prophets and cultists. Among others, John Locke with the *Essay on Civil Government* (1690), Montesquieu with *The Spirit of the Laws* (1748), Rousseau with *The Social Contract* (1762), as well as the encyclopaedists, were gradually undermining, from an intellectual point of view, the absolutist edifice and propagating ideals that would serve as foundations for the American and French Revolutions at the end of the eighteenth century.

In the eighteenth century, at the same time that these two political arguments for and against absolutism were taking root, an important intellectual movement developed and was to have a profound impact upon thought, society, and politics. As early as the sixteenth century Humanism had been a cry of freedom against scholasticism and the annihilation of the teaching structures of the time, in a search for intellectual renewal. Now, in the eighteenth century, a new change was brought about, driven by an intellectual elite, which wished that the human spirit might be freed from the constraints that limited it, in order for it to reach reason by the means of enlightenment.

In the field of politics, some such as Locke advocated the right of subjects to insurrection in case of violation of natural rights by the sovereign. This was an argument that could be used to justify the overthrow of James II, the legitimate king, and the call of William of Orange to the throne of England in 1688. It was advocated in the following terms: 'The people [...] have, by a law antecedent and paramount to all positive laws of men, reserved that ultimate determination to themselves which belongs to all mankind, where there lies no appeal on earth, whether they have just cause to make their appeal to heaven'.[4] Most, however, considered that it was the all-powerful sovereign who could best secure respect for those rights. All the same, everyone, as a general rule, defended the suppression of serfdom (which had been occurring slowly since the end of feudalism), economic freedom, religious tolerance (arising from horror against the religious wars of the previous centuries, and various political decisions, such as the repeal of the Edict of Nantes by Louis XIV, which had led a large number of Protestants to seek refuge in the Netherlands and Overseas), the abolition of birth privileges in the name of

3 Chevalier, *Grandes Oeuvres*, p.73

4 John Locke, *Second Treatise of Government* (Indianapolis: Hackett Publishing Company, 1980), pp.87-88.

Manuel de Azevedo Fortes. Belonging to the Enlightenment movement, he was the author of the first treatise on logic that was entirely written in Portuguese: the *Lógica Racional Geométrica e Analítica* (Geometrical and Analytical Rational Logic), which was published in Lisbon in 1744. He attempted, throughout this work, to find a compromise between the philosophies of Locke and Descartes. Azevedo Fortes (1660-1749) was appointed Chief Engineer of the Kingdom in 1719 and also wrote the *Tratado do Modo mais fácil e exacto de fazer as Cartas Geographicas* (Treatise on the easiest and most accurate Way of producing Geographical Maps) of 1722 and *O Engenheiro Portuguez* (The Portuguese Engineer), a work in two volumes that was published in 1728 and 1729. (Painting attributed to Pierre Antoine Quillard, National Palace of Mafra)

the equality of rights, and the defence of property as the result of the inequality of talent.[5]

Considering all this, the situation of society and of the political ideas and structures in the mid-eighteenth century can be summarised as follows. The disappearance of the feudal structure highlighted the importance of the monarch and his connection to the people. This connection, and the development of the national languages that 'killed' Latin, fuelled nationalisms. With the exception of England and the United Provinces, which had important parliaments and assemblies, the European monarchies practiced absolutism. Several authors upheld absolutism, but others emerged who questioned the foundations for sovereign power and undermined it. The phenomenon of the Enlightenment led to a reanalysis of the sovereign's concerns and, given the degree of suspicion with which it looked at certain dogmatic positions and the authority of the Church, it underlines the importance of 'enlightened despotism'.

## Science and Technology

The second half of the second millennium was a turning point in the evolution of thought and science. Prior to that, man accepted in a natural way what he was allowed to observe, preferring not to worry and doubt: religion and dogma satisfied, in general terms, his curiosity. Man did not need to waste his anxiety in a search for certainty, since, with the cultural heritage he had received, the knowledge he possessed and his faith, he owned 'the truth'. At the turn of the second half of the millennium, an intellectual movement occurred that significantly altered this situation. This movement derived, on a first moment, from a new idea about the world, from the new worlds, from the awareness of other cultures, from the innovations offered by nature which had hitherto been unknown and, as Paul Valéry said, from the 'discovery of the finite world', which the Portuguese gradually revealed through their great adventure of exploration. Álvaro de Campos mentioned this discovery, which is at the origin of the scientific spirit, by stating that the Portuguese sailors 'saw after all no monsters or great depths, but wonderful beaches and stars still to be seen. What do the world's vaults hide in God's storefronts?'[6]

5 Corvisier, *História Universal*, p.388.

6 Frenando Pessoa, *Poesias de Álvaro de Campos, Obras Completas de Frenando Pessoa* (Lisboa: Ática, 1980), p.30.

While it is a fact that the movement of Counter-Reformation, given the unusual rigour with which it was enforced beyond the Pyrenees against anything that could harm the convictions of faith, isolated the Iberian Peninsula from the current of thought liberation that invaded Europe at that time, it is also true that nothing could halt this march to modernity anymore.

In a second moment, which was also one of destruction of old myths and beliefs that had been hitherto uncontested, Copernicus and Galileo 'discovered' that the Earth was not the centre of the Universe, but only one of its elements. Given the revolutionary content of this discovery, the Church was unwilling to acknowledge it. In a third moment, in the seventeenth century, Descartes engaged, in the *Discourse on the Method*, in concepts such as those of methodical doubt, mathematical reasoning, and man's ability to think and doubt, even while he did not abandon the mystical spirit. In doing so, he accelerated the decline of the focus on intellectual discipline which had characterised the Middle Ages and strengthened the birth of the scientific spirit by the desire to arrive at truth through reason.

The evolution of thought and the birth of the scientific spirit, as well as the dialectic which the latter created with religion, was of consequence in several domains and had an impact on the events of the second half of the eighteenth century, which was the period of the military campaign we are examining. Several new realities converged. Political thought evolved, which produced consequences in the exercise of authority and of the political structures, as already discussed. Developments in the domains of law and international relations were occurring, which produced consequences in the fields of diplomacy and war. New forms and techniques of production emerged in the areas of agriculture, manufacturing and the burgeoning industry. New metal alloys were found, which were to be important for various uses and in particular for the production of war material. Shipbuilding developed, which in turn sparked new research in the industrial domain. Combat doctrines at sea and on land improved, as the result of a search for greater effectiveness of military force.

## Expansion and Colonialism

The maritime expansion of Portugal and Spain in the fifteenth and sixteenth centuries revolutionised European thinking and global geopolitics, and marked the beginning of the phenomenon of globalisation which is so much talked about today (for its potentialities, dangers and challenges). This was particularly felt after the defeat of the 'Invincible Armada' in 1588. Thereafter, several European powers openly challenged the almost total hegemony and monopoly of the Iberian countries. The Netherlands and England were at the forefront of this dispute. This can be explained with respect to the Netherlands as a result of the fact that it had a highly pragmatic society, available wealth, and a great capacity and spirit of initiative to carry out commercial and maritime enterprises. The importance of maritime trade to the Netherlands was such that in the early years of the seventeenth century they built as many ships and had as many sailors as all the other European countries together.[7] As for England, the situation can be partly understood in view of the fact that the crown had great difficulties obtaining the Parliament's consent to increase taxes and therefore found that its support of corsairs (Elizabeth I invested large sums in them) and its imposition of customs duties to be could be effective ways of overcoming these difficulties.

These two states, which had long had the knowledge, the desire and the required practice for the development of their naval power, increased their fleets. They also began discussing with the Portuguese and the Spanish their presence and traffic in their respective hemispheres, which 'belonged' to the two Iberian powers according to the 1494 Treaty of Tordesillas, and interfering in the commercial routes through raids. In the second half of the sixteenth century, given the inability of the Portuguese to enforce their monopoly, the British practiced smuggling in the empire, dominated routes, and formed trading companies. The Dutch did the same, while focusing on the East, initially on the Indian Ocean and Southeast Asia and later on Japan. At a later stage, France joined the Netherlands and England, following the ironic question, which is attributed to Francis I, as to whether the division of the world between the Portuguese and the Spaniards, with the blessing of Pope Alexander VI, had already been contemplated in Adam's will. France also sought to partake of the riches of the East and the New World and to be present and settle in these regions.

This phenomenon of European expansion, presence, and influence in areas that were remote from the Old Continent was the natural consequence from policies of affirmation, wealth and power that pursued several aims. One of them was obtaining goods at a low cost, which could then be sold in Europe at very high profit margins. Another was obtaining raw materials that were needed for manufacturing. As early as the eighteenth century, with the first steps towards industrialisation, these would be viewed as crucial to increase the income of enterprises and the state. An additional aim was finding new markets and outlets for European products, which might lead to an increase in trade and wealth. Furthermore, the European powers wished to get hold of cheap human resources or labour, which the New World needed to develop local cultivation. Moreover, they wished to obtain coinage metals, which they needed in order to acquire goods that were essential for their well-being, development, and safety – as well as, very often, for ostentation, satisfaction of whims and luxury. Also, through these policies, they could attempt to deny to rival powers new means for supremacy and hegemony.

The discoveries, the creation of commercial factories and warehouses and the process of colonisation encouraged the displacement of people and the creation of settlements by the countries that exploited and controlled the places and territories that came under their grip. This was necessary not only to achieve dynamism and an enthusiasm for the practice of trade but also to guarantee and consolidate the colonial strongholds, which were subject to harassment by local people and to competition from other European powers. In addition,

7 Corvisier, *História Universal*, p.125.

settlement was considered as a response to the need of a large workforce for the labour-intensive cultures, although it was not satisfactory in this respect, the shortage of labour being easily met otherwise by the slave market.

The dimension of settlement varied according to interests and threats and included individuals who were more or less skilled and were often subject to persecutions of a religious and political character. These sections of the population carried with them, in addition to the cultures and traits of their original nationalities, many of the tensions and conflicts that ravaged Europe.

## Economy and Trade

There were also major changes in the economy and in trade in the mid-millennium. Prior to Vasco da Gama, the predominant form of economy was based on subsistence and barter and was focused on very restricted geographical spaces (around urban centres). It was only in certain privileged ports that a more intensive level of trade took place. This kind of trade involved Oriental products, which were traded in some Mediterranean cities; products from southern Europe, which circulated in Mediterranean ports and also in Atlantic ports up until the French coast; and products from the North, which were traded in the Baltic and in the sea and river ports of Northern Europe.

During the sixteenth century, the establishment of Portuguese factories along the African coast, and especially the exploitation of trade throughout the Indian Ocean and in the Far East, snatched the monopoly of the spices and products of those regions from Venice and Genoa. For this reason and due to the conquest and exploitation of America by the Spanish, the centre of gravity of the overseas trade left the Mediterranean and moved to Lisbon and Seville, with repercussions upon the economy of the Iberian countries and of the whole of Europe.

The monopoly policy of certain products, such as spices (which the House of India in Lisbon sold to Europe, in exchange for products needed in Portugal), as well as the control of the trade network of the Orient that had hitherto belonged to the Arabs, fuelled certain European manufacturing industries, intensified trade, and fuelled the economy. This impulse boosted the power of sovereigns, the luxury of the courts, the development of armament (by virtue of its connection to power), and reinforced the authority of the state. By highlighting the importance of currency in transactions, it also increased the will to obtain coinage metals. In fact, Christopher Columbus had already said, while predicting the importance of money and thinking about wealth and the purchase of indulgences, that 'gold is a treasure, and he who owns it has everything he needs in the world, and, much like it, also has the means of rescuing the souls from purgatory and of summoning them to paradise'.[8]

8 Corvisier, *História Universal*, p.66.

The Reformation, which was partly a consequence from the scandalous fact that the Church had enriched itself by issuing indulgences (an act that called into question its perspective of criticism of profit-seeking individuals), ultimately stimulated the development of a capitalist bourgeoisie and the economy of certain European regions. In fact, this position of the Church, as well as its condemnation of usury, which was an element of its anti-Semitic discourse and was the basis for persecutions endorsed by the Inquisition, led many Jews to leave the Iberian Peninsula. Their financial power and initiative in the regions to which they fled was an important element in the development of the countries that welcomed them. Simultaneously, as countries were growing more aware about the importance of keeping a favourable trade balance, mercantilist theory instigated states to develop national industries and encouraged them to grow certain crops and to obtain cash through customs duties.

At the end of the sixteenth century, Iberian dominance of the overseas trade was challenged by the creation of companies, such as Britain's Honourable East India Company and the Dutch Oost Indische Compagnie, with sovereign power over conquered lands, the right to own a navy and troops, and exemption from customs duties. These companies generated enormous profits, stimulated the economy and the development of their own countries, and produced a new shift in the centre of gravity of commercial activity, which now moved on to the oceanic and riverine harbours of England and the Netherlands. In the first half of the eighteenth century, France tried to follow on the heels of the successful English and Dutch companies and managed to set up trading posts in the Indian Ocean, Senegal, the Antilles and North America, but these lacked the projection and the dynamism which those companies had achieved.

The policy of the companies ranged from taking advantage of unoccupied land, particularly in the New World, to struggling with other powers already in place and plundering along the trade routes. However, although by the turn of the eighteenth century the Portuguese and Spanish Empires had become a shadow of what they had been in the sixteenth century, their presence and wealth in Central and South America were still very important.

The War of the Spanish Succession (1701-1714) allowed France to develop its maritime trade with Spanish America and in 1715, under the peace of Utrecht, the country managed to negotiate some trade agreements. Nevertheless, in 1720 France's banking institutions, which had fuelled its expansion, its confidence, and its wealth, underwent a bitter experience and France felt the need for a new drive that might allow it to assert itself in Europe and in the world.

Because British policy was subordinate to commercial interests and the expansion and consolidation of Britain's presence overseas required a strong navy, Britain engaged in developing it and became the leading maritime power in the world. However, at Utrecht, where a new balance between European powers had been sought, Britain had been granted the slave trade and a 'permit vessel'; an annual ship that was free from control by the 'House of Hiring' in Seville. This shows how, despite the undeniable British supremacy in trade and in the seas, the status of the Iberian countries in the New World was still significant.

Therefore, by the middle of the eighteenth century, from the economic and commercial point of view, Britain was thriving, France lagged far behind the British overseas dynamics, and the Iberian countries kept on pursuing trade on a scale that was both influential in terms of European development and the envy of other powers. As time went by and new ideas seeped in, the balance of power that had been achieved through the Peace of Utrecht proved to be precarious. Renewed conflict was brewing.

3

# Military Framework

## Tensions and War

The type of war that characterised the feudal era, the war between lords, was succeeded by another type that emerged as a consequence of the centralisation of power and the dilution of allegiance ties, and can be defined as a type of 'business among princes'. Yet, while some of the conflicts of the sixteenth and seventeenth centuries were grounded in religion, disputes between princes often occurred due to problems of succession. This was not a new rationale for war. For example, in Portugal it had been invoked during the reign of Fernando I, again after his death in 1383, and again and 1580. Now, however, conflict was more based on aspects related to the economy and power and was brought about by a range of situations as powers struggled for hegemony or over their borders. The novelty now was that a domino effect followed from the existence of coalitions and alliances, and the possibility arose of a war spreading to the whole of Europe or a significant part of it.

The time had not yet come when war would become a conflict between nations, a development heralded by the growth of nationalism that the French Revolution turned into a reality. Nevertyeless, at the beginning of the eighteenth century, nationalisms were emerging, the technical means for making war were evolving, and diplomacy was being more frequently used as a way to achieve objectives without resorting to war. However, the legend '*ultima ratio regis*' was engraved on Louis XIV's cannon, which suggests that, while politics and diplomacy could try to resolve the internal and external conflicts of the state, cannon, a symbol of military power, would always be the 'last argument of the king'. The best use of diplomacy was not yet the search to prevent war from occurring at all, which is an idea that only took significant steps in the current age.

By the eighteenth century, out of the four Horsemen of the Apocalypse of St. John, two had been practically vanquished, but the other two boldly advanced through the world. The plague, that scourge that had so often reaped millions of lives in Europe, had disappeared. Famine had declined significantly, due to the introduction of high-yield crops brought in from the New World. Maize, which originated in America and arrived in Portugal in the sixteenth century, spread throughout the whole of Europe as the result of its abundant yields, which were much higher than those of local cultures (in the order of 100 to 1). The cultivation of maize helped overcome hunger crises, which always happened during the years of low wheat production. Thus, famine had become confined to very localised areas and to particularly adverse circumstances such as devastation from war, plunder, or rural exodus.

In contrast, war, besides continuing to be a cause of death and destruction, had widened its scope and had become bloodier. As for conquest, willingness to resort to it spread throughout most of the European countries, which, following the path of the Spanish *conquistadors*, imposed their presence, and practiced colonisation and war, in order to enjoy riches which up until the 1500s had been unknown or inaccessible to them. The War of the Spanish Succession, at the turn of the eighteenth century, led to the alignment of European countries and to the extension of their struggle to the colonies. Conflict between two states aroused the solidarity of others and the new overseas territories were included in their disputes, as areas of interest, as places of intended sovereignty and exploitation, as sources of power, and as bargaining chips.

## Military Force

Military force benefitted from technological achievements as the eighteenth century opened, and underwent important organisational and operational changes. The main innovation in terms of weaponry was the introduction of the socket bayonet which, when fitted to firearms, did not prevent firing. This enabled combatants to perform two functions which, until then, had required two specialised individuals, the musketeer and the pikeman. This was a profound change with repercussions in terms of army organisation, battle formation, command and discipline, and the preparation of combatants. In the middle of the sixteenth century the ratio between arquebusiers and pikemen had been of one to five. The introduction of the plug bayonet had then dismissed the need for a large number of pikemen and had led to a relative balance in the numbers of combatants. However, the use of socket bayonets totally dismissed the need for pikemen, as now a single combatant could perform both functions.

Organisationally, the battalion became the fundamental unit of combat. Most commonly in Contenental Europe, the regiment was split into two battalions. It should be noted that the 'importance of the battalion resulted from its unitary characteristics, from its operational and logistical capacity, and also from the fact that it was the highest unit in which it was still possible for the commander to exercise his command by using his own voice and by looking his men in the eye'.[1] Another important new development, which was influential with respect to the armies and the war, was the emergence of

1 António Barrento, 'Introdução: O Exército Português e os Seus Generais: Das Invasões Francesas à Queda da Monarquia (1807-1910)', in *Os Generais do Exército Português* (Lisboa: Biblioteca do Exército, 2005), Vol.II, p.30.

a type of artillery that was mobile enough to be able to follow the march and the manoeuvres of armies.

The organisational ancestor of national armies was that of Gustavus Adolphus of Sweden, recognised for its effectiveness in the Thirty Years War. However, economic constraints, ranging from demand for labour to cover the needs of agricultural and industrial production (required for welfare, mercantilism, and colonisation) to the fact that the cost of military units now had to be fully supported by the royal treasury, prevented the formation of large armies. However, better direction of available revenues helped improve the effectiveness of the existing forces. The need to maintain societal norms predicated the recruitment of officers from amongst the nobility and of soldiers from the fringes of society, as a result of which losses through desertion often exceeded those due to casualties in combat.

The above-mentioned economic and social circumstances made it costly and difficult to obtain soldiers, and thus military units, who were both well instructed and effective. In turn, this led army commanders to avoid battle unless circumstances were particularly favourable to them. As a consequence, campaigns dragged on and became a 'game' of displacement of forces, for the purpose of achieving (or depriving the adversary of) the favourable conditions to fight a battle.

From the tactical point of view, the objective was for combat formations to take advantage of the increase in firepower due to the improvement of individual weapons, the suppression of pikemen, and the added value of artillery. Hence the importance linear infantry formations of multiple ranks that could guarantee continuous fire (since loading guns was still time-consuming), and of discipline in formations and movements. The virtues of a line did not prevent a quarrel over the advantages of linear order and deep order, since the former stressed the density of the fires and the second the reiteration of the efforts. Frederick II of Prussia's 'oblique order' was nothing more than the use of high combat potential in that portion of the battlefield where the main effort was to be made, whilst retaining linear formations on the remaining front. However, the debate between the various schools, which occupied the military thought of the eighteenth century, was only part of the dialectic between fire and shock, defence and attack, and line and column. This debate it still followed today, in tactics, when attitudes are compared and modes of action are analysed.

Nevertheless, in the organisational and operational spheres, the model now approached that of the Prussian army, with highly trained combatants, rigid combat formations and discipline, added support of fire from a mounted artillery that was able to follow the movements of the cavalry, and the development of a light infantry, which possessed initiative and acted in open formations (a skill in which the Portuguese would prove themselves particularly adept in the Peninsular War of the early nineteenth century).

Frederick II, the philosopher-king, a follower of the political ideas of Diderot's *Encyclopaedia*, never failed to incarnate the military soul of his kingdom and soon understood that poor and lean Prussia could only rest safely within the fortress of a good army to which the nobility might supply the officers, the bourgeoisie the money, and the people the soldiers. Deeply

Infantry in the reign of João V. Infantry battalion with 10 companies, including one of grenadiers. The major is on horseback in front of the battalion, the colonel is immediately behind the grenadiers and the lieutenant-colonel closes the formation. The flags and the drummers are in the centre of the formation. The drawing seems to show that the battalion was already formed in three ranks. (Engraving from the book by Bento Gomes Coelho, *Milícia pratica e manejo de infantaria…* (Practical militia and infantry practice) Lisboa, 1740)

learned, investigative and critical, he put all his effort to remedying the defects he had observed in his army, by increasing its organic cohesion, its means of attack, and its offensive power. By encouraging exertion through rewards and by imposing strict discipline by means of severe corporal punishments, he generated new concepts of military honour, esprit de corps, professional value and allegiance to the sovereign, all of which were imponderable factors that brought about new characteristics, a kind of own soul, to the permanent armies of his time. Moreover, from his understanding that the best strategy should be offensive in character, he taught that attack initiative forced the enemy to regulate his movements by those of the attacker, which meant placing him in a situation of inferiority. In addition, he recognised that the essential aim of an army in campaign should be the army of the adversary and not its fortresses, that he who wished to preserve everything could not preserve anything, and that, in order to engage in a battle, as many resources should be put together as possible. These pre-Napoleonic maxims already presaged the absolute war of movement and shock, in which a battle aimed at destroying the armies of the enemies should be the supreme purpose of a campaign.[2]

2 Carlos Selvagem, *Portugal Militar. Compêndio de História Militar e Naval de Portugal. Desde as Origens do Estado Portucalense até ao Fim da Dinastia de Bragança* (Lisboa: Imprensa Nacional, 1931), pp.472-473.

## The Seven Years War

As a result of the peace of Aix-la-Chapelle signed in 1748, which put an end to the War of the Austrian Succession that had involved several European powers, Maria Theresa was recognised as Empress, despite the amputations which the Habsburg Empire had suffered in this conflict. However, in 1756 the Empress entered into an alliance with France, Russia, Sweden, and Saxony, for the purpose of recovering Silesia, which Frederick II of Prussia had seized as early as 1740 (upon the death of Emperor Charles VI) and which Maria Theresa had relinquished to him, together with the County of Glatz, in 1742, in order to obtain peace. Britain, which in the War of the Austrian Succession had supported Maria Theresa, was now on the side of Prussia, in search of continental equilibrium. This led it to fight against the colonial and economic power of France, which has been growing since the Peace of Utrecht. Thus, in the middle of the eighteenth century, a large part of the European powers became involved in a new war which, given its duration, was later called the Seven Years War (1756-1763).

Two blocks emerged, with Britain and Prussia on one side, and France, Austria, and Russia on the other. The two Iberian countries initially affirmed their neutrality with respect to this conflict. Prussia intended to solidify its position in Germany and in Europe, and ultimately succeeded. This was the work of military genius Frederick II. France, which, despite some setbacks, had succeeded, through the Peace of Utrecht, in confirming its conquests of the seventeenth century, wished to maintain its presence throughout the oceans and colonies, including in North America, where its area of influence extended from Louisiana to Canada. Britain, as a maritime and economic power with worldwide reach, disputed the strength and the ambitions of the other European powers, especially France: preventing France from reaching a degree of hegemony in the European continent was a major British goal.

The neutrality which the Iberian countries so much wished to keep did not prevent English ships from dropping anchor at their harbours, nor from sailing along the peninsular coast and from causing serious impediments to French navigation and damage to its navy. For example, in August 1761, two English ships which had left the port of Lisbon became involved, close to Cape Finisterre, in a battle with three French ships on their way from Saint-Domingue. This combat resulted in the seizure of one of the French ships and produced more than 200 dead among their crews.[3]

It was disasters such as this and 'the case of Lagos', of which more later, that led Louis XV to seek, in 1761, with the Family Compact, to attract Spain and Portugal to the Bourbon coalition against Britain. This policy was only successful with respect to Spain, but brought about Portugal's entry into the war and the invasion of Portuguese territory by a Franco-Spanish Army.

3 For a description of this combat and of its consequences, see S.J. Luz Soriano, *História do Reinado de El-Rei D. José* (Lisboa: Tipografia Nacional, 1867), Vol.I, pp.475-476.

4

# Genesis of the Conflict

## Environment in Portugal

From the Portuguese perspective, it is necessary to mention some aspects about the reign of João V and about the influence that the Marquis of Pombal exerted on the reign of the King, given their connection with the events of the Seven Years War.

João V reigned in French-inspired monarchist absolutism and justified the centralisation, pomp and luxury of his governance through the royal fifth (*quinto real*), a 20 percent tax which he imposed on the gold from Brazil. After the War of the Spanish Succession, which occurred at the very beginning of his reign, the long peace that followed led the monarch to focus his interest on religiosity, erudition, the arts, and the ostentation of wealth as forms of demonstration of power. Issues of security and defence only deserved marginal attention. As Latino Coelho put it, the King 'had imitated the splendour and the luxury of Louis XIV for his court, but neither his character nor his destiny had inclined him to follow the warlike adventures of his happy model'.[1]

While it is true that military ordinances and regiments were created in the reign of João V, and that an effort was made to put forward legislation aimed at setting up a modern army that might reach the standards that were current in Europe, all the work that was done did not produce its desired purpose. 'After the War of Succession, the regiments, which were short of staff, vegetated miserably in the idle life of the garrisons. The exercises, especially those that involved firing, were a very rare and extraordinary event in each unit. Even the handling of weapons, which was carried out in a uniform, perfect way even among troops that had had poor firing training, was incoherent and irregular... The soldiers did not receive, during the long peace that followed the War of Succession, the slightest training about campaign service'.[2] In addition, the reorganisation of 1715 resulted in a significant reduction of the units. True, military academies emerged, but

1 J.M. Latino Coelho, *História Política e Militar de Portugal* (Lisboa: Imprensa Nacional, 1874), Vol.I, p.1.

2 Latino Coelho, *História Política e Militar*, Vol.III, pp.46-47.

the 'theorical teaching of the military sciences did not extend beyond some faint rudiments'.[3]

Portugal did not have the army and the strength it needed for its safety and for the standing it aimed to have in Europe and overseas. Its infantry did not reach 8,000 men in 1735 and, instead of preparing for war, it was involved in transporting materials for building the Palace of Mafra. Military wages were systematically paid in delay and desertions happened permanently. The generals and senior officers usually valued not competence but illustrious blood.

A situation of military decline was clear, following the excellent behaviour of the Portuguese army in the War of the Spanish Succession and, in 1717, the remarkable action of the Portuguese fleet in the Battle of Matapan agsinst the Turks. It should be noted, however, that in the 1720s and 1730s the Portuguese naval and land units responded effectively against British and Dutch interventions in Cabinda and São João da Mina, as well as in its defence of some forts in North Africa. Moreover, in the 1740s, Portuguese military action in India under the Viceroy of India, the Marquis of Castelo-Novo, was highly successful. Several factors contributed to this success. The Viceroy received support from the political leadership in Portugal, in response to his requests for help. Also, an organisational and operational system was in place that proved effective to carry out naval, amphibious, and land operations when these were necessary. Five carracks and ten infantry companies arrived in Goa, which allowed the Portuguese to conquer fortified settlements inland, so as to guarantee Goa's defence. Most importantly, the Viceroy was a valiant chieftain and an experienced combatant, whose services were also recognised by João V when he awarded him the title of Marquis of Alorna.

When the King died in 1750, after a prolonged illness, the Portuguese army was, in the words of Latino Coelho, 'just a nominal force', although several incidents with Spain and France had occurred during his reign, which might have served as reminders of the need to strengthen the existing force. These showed that in the future relations with these two countries would not be free from tensions and dangers. Indeed, in 1762, conflict spiralled and led these countries to war against Portugal.

The possibility of war was heightened by Portugal's geographic location and geostrategic situation, as well as by the tensions that existed between the British Empire and the Bourbon monarchies, between maritime and continental power. Portugal, a coastal country which could project its power onto other continents by the sea, found itself in the uncomfortable situation of being a frontier, an area of interest, a field for manoeuvres and a source of discussion between the great European maritime and continental powers. Miguel Torga's verse from the *Canticle of Man*, which reads 'when time comes for me to decide, look for me in the dunes where I will be split between the sea and the land', can be used as an image for Portugal's situation, by extending the initial meaning from the individual to the collective and from well-being to security. As it happened, Portugal was at a crossroads and at the frontier between these powers. It was an isobar of their capacities and intentions,

3 Latino Coelho, *História Política e Militar*, Vol.III, p.51.

as a strip of territory that was destined to suffer from turbulence. Because geography is tyrannical and persistent, it was not the first time that Portugal faced this dilemma. It would not be the last. With Napoleon the situation was still more dramatic because of the intensity of the struggle that resulted from the vigour of the clashing ideologies.[4]

José I of Portugal (1714-1777) was enthroned in 1750 following the death of João V. He appointed Carvalho e Melo as Secretary of State of Foreign Affairs and War, who was and was awarded the title of Count of Oeiras in 1759, following his intervention after the Earthquake of 1755 and the regicide attempt. (Unsigned and undated painting, Institute of the National Archives – Torre do Tombo, Lisbon)

During the reign of José I, who succeeded his father João V, an important player emerged: Sebastião José de Carvalho e Mello, who was Count of Oeiras and later became Marquis of Pombal. A controversial figure in Portuguese history, about whom the worst and the best that can be said about a statesman was and is said, he won the trust of José I and directed the affairs of the kingdom with authority, intuition, and in conformity with the new teachings from the Enlightenment to which he had been exposed through foreign travel and contact with the intellectuals of his time. A text written about him during his lifetime read that 'Sebastião José de Carvalho e Mello was a man whom José I made his Secretary on the day that he succeeded to the Portuguese crown, and that in such a way he was able to dominate his will, and to make himself respected by all the vassals, as the King did not seem to have a free mind'. It added that he was endowed 'with a good capacity but was lacking in religion and charity, and was inhuman, barbarous, cruel, unfaithful, and excessively ambitious'.[5]

For Latino Coelho, as Sebastião José entered political sphere and was

> ...called to exercise a quasi-unlimited power, the very pitiful situation of the kingdom stimulated his zeal and showed him that, as his enterprise, to which he committed his bold chest, would be all the more arduous, his glory would be all the greater and the laurels of his triumph all the more attractive [...]. Just like some of the most untroubled statesmen of the preceding reign, who had been educated in the school of politics and in the company of foreigners [...], he returned to his homeland to wretchedly confirm the inferences from an extremely sad confrontation between Portugal and the most prosperous nations, in which it had lived. [...] He had a suitable talent, a creative spirit, and an understanding honed by readings, sharpened by journeys, and capable of new and risky ventures.[6]

4 António Barrento, 'O Exército Português Antes e Depois do Conde de Lippe', in António Barrento, *Reflexões sobre Temas Militares* (Lisboa: Instituto de Altos Estudos Militares, 2000), Vol.II, p.264.

5 Luz Soriano, *História do Reinado de El-Rei D. José*, Vol.I, p.196n.

6 Latino Coelho, *História Política e Militar*, Vol.I, pp.2, 15-17.

Sebastião José de Carvalho e Melo (1699-1782) became a member of the Royal Academy of Portuguese History in 1733 and an ambassador in London from 1739 and in Vienna from 1745. In the Austrian capital he wed Maria Leonor Ernestina Daun, daughter of the famous Austrian Marshal Daun. He was appointed Secretary of State of Foreign Affairs and War in August 1750 and Secretary of State of the Kingdom in 1756. His political achievements were recognized though the award of the titles of Count of Oeiras in 1759 and Marquis of Pombal in 1769. (Painting attributed to Joana de Salitre, City Museum, Lisbon)

Lúcio de Azevedo made a more distant analysis. Mentioning how challenging it was 'to raise the reputation of the country abroad, to strengthen the authority inland, to restore the financial situation, and also to ensure mercantile traffic with the colonies, and to revive the decadent industries by means of adequate measures',[7] he recognised the virtues and the positive aspects of the minister of José I, without however denying his flaws.

The earthquake of 1755, a terrible tragedy of enormous dimension that plunged Portugal into mourning and caused consternation throughout Europe, tested Sebastião José's capacity for organisation and decision, as well as his determination. Although Portugal was then dominated by anachronistic superstitions and institutions, as Voltaire mentioned in *Candide*, this did not prevent the minister of José I from taking the necessary measures and from overcoming, with tenacity and vision, this calamitous situation.

An attempted attack on the King on 3 September 1758, under circumstances that were far from clear, produced a severe response that some considered a correct reaction against a crime of lèse-majesté and others viewed as an expression of the diabolical spirit of the future marquis, who thus subdued a section of the nobility that resisted despotic rule. This fact demonstrated determination in solving the affairs of the country and of the state but lends itself to discordant interpretations about Sebastião José.

The administration of the Count of Oeiras revealed a deeper concern with the army from the beginning, and some legislative measures were taken to improve it. However, the need for troops after the earthquake, and the feeling of insecurity that was generated by the attempted attack, showed that army was not in a position to ensure the defence of the country, in terms of organisation, readiness or discipline. A grotesque example of this, which was referred to by foreigners, was related to the delays in the payment of wages and to the existing situation of indiscipline. It was the fact that Portuguese soldiers asked for alms even when they were in their sentry post.[8] Although these situations possibly occurred with troops of the *Ordenança*, and not with the first-line enlisted soldiers, is it still unfortunate that this should have happened at all.

Later, as it became obvious that Portugal could not remain neutral in relation to the war that had been raging since 1756, especially under the pressure that arose from the Family Compact, the Count of Oeiras insisted on the need to obtain support from British forces. Furthermore, he issued decrees aimed at allowing the Portuguese army to quickly obtain the human and material resources it needed. A particularly important problem was the lack of a qualified military leadership and he was aware of the difficulty in finding someone in Portugal with the necessary knowledge, ability to command and experience. In this context, he identified the Count of Lippe as a much-needed military commander who would enable the army to grow and reorganise under an improved leadership.

---

7 J. Lúcio de Azevedo, *O Marquez de Pombal e a sua Época* (Lisboa: Clássica Editora, 1909), p.112.

8 Latino Coelho, *História Política e Militar*, Vol.III, p.112.

Admiral Edward Boscawen (1711-1761) was appointed commander of the British fleet in the Mediterranean in 1759, and pursued the French fleet, under the command of Admiral de La Clue, as it was on its way from Toulon to the English Channel where it aimed to support an attempt by France to invade Great Britain. Both fleets met off the coast of Lagos in the Algarve on 17 August 1759, during which encounter the French naval forces lost five ships. (Unsigned and undated painting, National Maritime Museum, Greenwich)

## The Case of Lagos

In response to setbacks elsewhere, France developed a strategy of making a landing in Britain, much as Spain had already attempted at the end of the sixteenth century with its 'Invincible Armada'. Through this initiative, the centre stage of combat shifted to British territory, which meant that the British were prevented from continuing to exploit their developed naval power to their advantage. In July 1759, in an anticipatory manoeuvre, the British destroyed the transport fleet that was being prepared in the port of Le Havre. Those parts of the French fleet in Brest and Dunkirk were blockaded, whilst Admiral Boscawen was tasked with dealing with the French fleet in the Mediterranean.

On 17 August 1759, in the context of this manoeuvre of neutralisation of French naval power, the British fleet under Boscawen's command defeated a French fleet near the Algarve coast. In this fight, three ships were burnt, two were captured, numerous casualties occurred, and part of the crews, which had gathered on boats, sought refuge on the coast. After landing, the French tried to assemble in Lagos but ultimately, even on land, kept being persecuted and fired at by the British. These British actions represented an attack on Portuguese sovereignty and on the policy of neutrality that Portugal had sought to pursue in this conflict. The French ambassador to Lisbon, the Count of Merle, first thanked the Portuguese authorities for their treatment of the shipwrecked, but, in September, urged to do so by the French government, he protested against the offence against Portugal's neutrality, since the attack had taken place in Portuguese waters, two French ships had been captured, and the crews, even ashore, had been targeted by the British.[9]

Relations between the French ambassador and the Count of Oeiras were characterised by reciprocal antipathy, which did not facilitate the development of the diplomatic action that was needed to solve this difficult political problem. In this context, given how right France was, the

9 Lúcio de Azevedo, *O Marquez de Pombal*, p.259.

Portuguese Secretary of Foreign Affairs, Luís da Cunha Manuel, responded evasively to the complaints put forward by the French ambassador. However, José I, who was aware of the excesses that had been committed by the British, determined that reparation be sought from London. The British minister in Lisbon, Mr Hay, therefore expressed King George's concern about this affair and his desire to know 'whether His Majesty's ships had sufficiently respected the coasts of Portugal; whether the French ships had not been captured with offense to the territorial jurisdiction of His High Majesty'. William Pitt, Secretary of State and de factor head of the British government, feared that this incident might bring Portugal closer to France and urged Hay to apologise, adding that 'if the circumstances for grievance are of sufficient magnitude, so much desire does the King feel to give more public and ostentatious satisfaction to the sovereign of Portugal that I think there will be no doubt to send him to this effect an extraordinary embassy'.[10] He added, however, that the captured ships would not be returned nor would the actions of the Admiral be disavowed

William Pitt (1708-1778) was appointed Minister of Foreign Affairs and War in 1756, under the title 'Secretary of State for the Southern Department', under the cabinets firstly of the Duke of Devonshire and secondly of the Duke of Newcastle. He was obliged to resign in 1761 as he proposed the declaration of war against Spain after the conquest of Canada from France. War was declared in 1762, just as he had proposed. In 1766 he set up a government and George III awarded him the titles of Earl of Chatham and Viscount Pitt. (Painting carried out in the studio of R. Brompton, National Portrait Gallery)

While the Count of Merle continued to complain and added other offences that had been committed against a French ship near Viana do Castelo, Britain sent a special ambassador to Lisbon. This ambassador, Lord Kinnoul, arrived on 3 March 1760 with three ships and the Count of Oeiras presented a note requiring the delivery of the seized vessels. This demand caused embarrassment to the British government, which, having already shown no intention of delivering them, avoided a clear statement of refusal, because it was offensive to Portugal.

On 21 March, Lord Kinnoul was received in a royal audience, in which he formally declared regret for what had happened in Lagos and reiterated the friendship of the British sovereign. This position satisfied the court and the Count of Oeiras, to the extent that the latter wrote that the declaration had been 'a manifest and lasting pledge of affection between the two courts'.[11] While this left the Count of Oeiras satisfied, given the reiteration of British friendship which might be necessary to Portugal in case of conflict, it did nothing to prevent the French ambassador from insisting on the return of the ships. This insistence led Luís da Cunha Manuel, while avoiding the

10 Pitt to Hay, 12 September 1759, quoted in Lúcio de Azevedo, *O Marquez de Pombal*, pp.262-263.

11 Count of Oeiras to Kinnoul, 26 March 1760, quoted in Lúcio de Azevedo, *O Marquez de Pombal*, p.267.

problem, to emphasise the existing family connection between the French and Portuguese sovereigns and the good relations with France (relations which were actually anything but and had even been made worse due to protocol issues related to the coming of Lord Kinnoul).

In May, given the attitudes and the expressed grievances by the Count de Merle, the government of Portugal complained about him to Versailles, and the Count of Oeiras, convinced that France wanted a pretext to declare war on Portugal, asked Britain for help. Britain reaffirmed its old alliance but suggested that Portugal should develop and organise its own military forces.[12]

Upon the death of Fernando VI of Spain in August 1759, who had followed a policy of neutrality and peace, relations with Spain also underwent moments of tension. First, the new King of Spain, Carlos III, brother of Mariana Victoria, wife of José I, began to demand the repeal of the Treaty of Boundaries in South America (which had not been implemented on the Portuguese side due only to resistance from the Indians). Nor did the Spanish wish to give up their claim to Colónia do Sacramento, on the River Plate, which had been awarded to Portugal udner the Treaty of Utrecht but which Spain wished to recover. Indeed, it has bene argued that 'the real cause of the conflict derived from the off-limit possessions in the New World, which had been tolerated for so long by the kings of Spain since Carlos V'.[13] Second, the marriage of Prince Pedro to his niece, Maria Francisca, Princess of Brazil, and future Queen Maria I, happened just one month after the Spanish ambassador had, in February 1761, requested the hand of the Princess for Prince Luís of Spain.

Despite the existing tension with Spain, it was France that the Count of Oeiras most feared and so he insisted with the Portuguese representative in London, Martinho de Melo e Castro, to guarantee British assistance in case Portugal could not maintain its position of neutrality (which had been affected by the events of Lagos) in relation to the conflict that had divided the main European powers for five years. However, when in 1761 France seemed to desire to secure peace with Britain, it became more important to obtain British support, a fact that led the Count of Oeiras to insist that aid be guaranteed to Portugal in case of aggression. The concern of the Portuguese government also increased because of the deterioration of relations between Spain and Britain.

On 15 August 1761, France and Spain signed the Family Compact, which Carlos III also wished to impose upon his brother-in-law, José I. Were this Spanish alliance with Portugal to be struck, it would bring about the enmity and hostility of Britain and would certainly result in the weakening, or even the loss, of the Portuguese empire. Were the alliance not to be formed, Portugal would once again engage in a war with neighbouring Spain, which was now an ally of France. France and its minister, Choiseul, anticipated 'that the war with Portugal, whatever the outcome, would always be of benefit to

12 Pitt to Lord Kinnoul, quoted in Lúcio de Azevedo, *O Marquez de Pombal*, p.270.

13 Anon., *Historia de España* (Barcelona: Instituto Gallach de Librería y Ediciones, 1943), Vol.V, p.79.

The son of Filipe V, King of Spain, and Isabel Farnésio, Duchess of Parma, Carlos III (1716-1788) succeeded to the throne upon the death of his half-brother Fernando VI who had no descendants. He was obliged to renounce to the throne of Naples, which he had governed since 1734, and signed the Family Compact with Louis XV of France in 1761. (Painting by Anton Raphael Mengs, Municipal Museum, Madrid)

France. Castella would gain at least the Colony of Sacramento, and perhaps some territory from the south of Brazil. In any case Choiseul took desired retaliation from the Portuguese Court'.[14]

The French and Spanish diplomatic representatives, fearing British action against the fleet of the Indies on its return to Spain (a trip that ended only in November) and sensing how difficult it would be to displace the forces that had been prepared to invade the North of Portugal, delivered a memorandum to Luís da Cunha Manuel only later in March. In this document they explained the wishes of their respective governments.

14 Lúcio de Azevedo, *O Marquez de Pombal*, p.281.

## The Memoranda

In this context, here are summarised some brief excerpts from the memoranda that were delivered to the Portuguese Court by the ambassadors of Spain and France, Don José Torrero and Jacob O'Dunne respectively, as well as from the reply to those that was made by Luís da Cunha Manuel. They are particularly relevant to understand the circumstances, the arguments, the complaints, and the reasons of each country, as well as the conflict that flared up.[15]

From the Memorandum of 16 March 1762:

> ... As both the monarchs of France and Spain found themselves in a situation whereby they needed to sustain a war against the British, they found it convenient and necessary to establish several mutual obligations and other indispensable measures, in order to try to contain the pride which had inspired the British nation with the ambitious project of being despotic in the seas, and consequently in all the overseas trade...
>
> ... One is to try to bring the most faithful King to their offensive and defensive alliance, so that he can soon join His Majesties for the same purpose, as one should expect from what is his duty to himself and to his kingdom, since his vassals suffer even more than the other nations from the yoke...
>
> ... It would be unfair for Spain and France to sacrifice themselves for something which Portugal is as much or more interested in; and for this power, instead of helping them, to make it impossible for them to achieve their purpose, as would happen by enriching and encouraging the enemy by keeping its trade running and its ports open...
>
> ... They ask the most faithful King [...] to declare himself united with His Catholic and Very Christian Majesties, in the current war against the British, while breaking its dealings and communication with this power, a common enemy to the three...
>
> ... How much more glorious and more useful it is for the most faithful King that a Catholic King of so immediate kinship, belonging to a neighbourhood of states in Europe and America that may succour each other and easily, is his ally, rather than the British nation, which is incapable, given its arrogance, to treat any other in equal terms...

In delivering this document, the ambassadors stressed that they received instructions to obtain a 'clear, decisive and categorical' reply within four days.

From the Portuguese reply of 20 March:

> ... There being the wish that the most faithful majesty, adopting in common the same motivations, should declare himself united offensively and defensively with his Catholic and Very Christian majesties for the said war, breaking all dealings

15 The original documents are at the National Library of Portugal, Cod. 1468, pp. 108-116. These excerpts are taken from copies of these at the Military Historical Archive. See documents *Exposições respeitantes às negociações entre os soberanos...*, DIV/1/7/1/31, and *Sem razão de entrarem em Portugal as tropas* castelhanas..., 1/7/5/19. The full text is reproduced in Luz Soriano, *História do Reinado de El-Rei D. José*, Vol.I, pp.503-523.

and communication with the British… and declaring the Catholic King on the aforesaid, that, before sending to this court the above-mentioned memorandum, he had made his troops march to the borders of this kingdom…

… There being, with the crown of Britain, old alliances, which have for so many years been uninterrupted, which are purely defensive and as such innocent, and which have been rendered public by so many and solemn treaties; and the crown of Portugal not having suffered from Britain any immediate offense…

… The above moral impossibilities, which lie outside the scope of decision of the most faithful monarch, could prevent him from entering the league, which has just been proposed to him; and you will see, furthermore, that it will also be impossible to carry out anything through the ports of this kingdom that even remotely may cause the slightest harm to his Catholic majesty, in violation of the firm neutrality that has been systematically pursued by this court…

From the Memorandum of 1 April:

… The impediments, put forward by His Most Faithful Majesty to the offensive and defensive attitudes, which his Catholic and Very Christian majesties propose to him, on the basis of defensive alliances with the Court of London are neither invincible nor founded. These alliances are also not as innocent as they appear. The impediments are not invincible, because everything must yield to the reason of shaking off the yoke, when there is a power that wants to dominate another, which is what the power of Britain tries and had much strived for with the power of Portugal…

… What greater offense can there be than for an English fleet to have chased a French fleet in a port of Portugal? That is enough for His Most Faithful Majesty to have a right to declare war against His British Majesty. […] And alliances are not innocent although they are called purely defensive…

… Those islanders would not insult all of maritime Europe and would let all of them enjoy their possessions and take their part in the trade, if in Portugal the source of their riches were closed to them. Consequently, Portugal renders them the means to war, and the alliance is offensive…

… They repeat to His Most Faithful Majesty all that they exposed in their memorandum of 16 March; they insist on the request which it contains; and they declare that, without any further document or consent, the Spanish troops close to the borders will enter into Portugal, with the sole purpose of advancing until they stop its ports from being at the disposal of the enemy…

From the Portuguese reply of 5 April:

… And declaring that, without any further document or consent from his most faithful majesty, the Spanish troops that are close to the borders of these kingdoms will enter into Portugal to occupy and close their ports…

Neither can one convincingly state that the treaties, which have existed for so long between this crown and that of Britain, are offensive, on the basis of the notion that they facilitate the commerce of Portugal to Britain…

… As to what happened to the ships of Mr. Lacloue's fleet on the Algarve coast, one cannot fail to recall that, [Portugal] having received from the King of Great

Britain such a compelling reparation with respect to the decorum of the fortress, in the vicinity of which some of those vessels were seised [...], it considered more natural to wait until the friendship of his British majesty might act upon those pressing diligences, so as to restore the aforementioned ships may be restored in due time, than to undertake to obtain their restitution by means of an untimely war...

... However, in the unforeseen case of the arrival of Spanish troops in Portugal [...], the monarch, who cannot evade making use of all possible means for its indispensable defence, without causing offense to the divine law, the natural law, and the law of the people and without causing universal scandal, has given orders that his own forces are used in Portugal's defence and that they may be joined to those of its allies: seeking, necessarily, to thus sustain the same neutrality which has always been and still is now his firm and sole objective...

## From the Memorandum of 23 April

... They put an end to the negotiation, which together they have undertaken and followed to bring His Most Faithful Majesty to the party that upholds his true interest...

... [His Most Faithful Majesty] having preferred the resistance against the entrance of the Spanish troops as enemies to their admission as friends, and consequently the enmity to the friendship of his Catholic and Very Christian majesties, [...] they hope you will deign to supply them with the necessary passports so that they can then retire each to their own courts.

Lisbon, 23 April 1762 = Don Joseph Torrero = Jaques Bernard O'Dunne.

## From the Portuguese reply of 25 April

... The actual break which the allied ministers have just confessed now by such clear and manifest words did not cause him the slightest novelty: having seen that the first opening to this (regrettable) negotiation consisted in notifying his most faithful majesty by means of the first memorandum of 16 March, that, without any previous report to him, the Courts of Paris and Madrid decided to turn the neutral kingdom of Portugal into a theatre of a war; to subject his most faithful majesty to calmly watch his provinces and ports be occupied by the Spanish armies; to inform him that it was with the aforesaid purpose that these armies were already stationed on the borders of this kingdom; to add to all this that he should, at the same time, not only infringe all the treaties of peace and commerce with the crown of Britain, but also declare an offensive war against it...

... Finally, His Most Faithful Majesty understands that he has such a right to defend his kingdom from invasions that any individual will lawfully and necessarily defend his own house against whoever wishes to enter it without his consent.

And his majesty concentrating on this single point of naturally defending the neutrality and peace of his kingdoms, ports, and subjects, he will do whatever he can to assemble his forces and those of his allies, in case he is under attack in spite of everything that has been mentioned...

# 5

# Forces

## Military Situation in Portugal

Lúcio de Azevedo portrayed the military situation and the state of the Portuguese forces in the years that preceded the country's entry into the Seven Years War in the following very bleak way:

> The borders were open, the forts were dismantled, the regiments were incomplete, the arms depots were empty. The officials were incompetent, many of whom were servants of noble families and were more occupied in working for their masters, who had promoted them, than in carrying out field or barrack service [...] the soldiers lacked training and discipline [...]. The naval forces were in the same state of abandonment. In everything concerning war, there was hardship, incapacity, carelessness [...] in November 1761, wages to the soldiers was eighteen months overdue. The Duke of Broglie, who was informed by spies, made a synthesis of all this and told Louis XV that the troops, which were few in number, were poorly paid, badly dressed, poorly armed, and in an even worse condition with respect to discipline, and were made up of individuals from the riffraff of the nation.[1]

This regrettable situation, which was corroborated at the time by both nationals and foreigners, was essentially due to the fact that for many years the political leadership had paid little attention to military affairs, as it had not thought that Portugal might become involved, in the short term, in another war. For this reason, the measures to improve the situation of the military force had been scarce and of limited effect.

During the reign of João V some legislation on military matters emerged, but it did not produce its desired effects. The idle life of the garrisons continued, characterised by the lack of firing and combat training, by shortage of funds, by constant desertions, and by permanent abuses to the regular functioning of the units and to the rules of discipline.[2]

This army was certainly not the best legacy that José I could have inherited. Its political leadership was unwilling, incapable and ignorant as to how to improve and adapt the military forces to the defensive needs of the country. Its higher officers were simply people of noble blood, while its lower ones were randomly chosen from family connections and among

Chief Engineer of the Kingdom, with the rank of lieutenant-general from 1754, Manuel da Maia (1677-1768) studied at the Fortification Class of Lisbon in 1701. Having participated in the Spanish Succession War, he was involved in the siege of Badajoz of 1708, was promoted to the rank of colonel in 1718 and to that of brigadier in 1738, at which point his pay doubled. In 1744 he was recognized as noble-cavalier of the Royal House. He participated in the construction of the Free Waters Aqueduct and in the reconstruction on Lisbon after the Earthquake.

Luís de Almeida Portugal (1729-1790), 5th Count of Avintes and 2nd Marquis of Lavradio, was promoted to the post of colonel of the regiment of Cascais in February 1761. Having been involved in the campaign of 1762, he was promoted to the post of brigadier in 1763. He was appointed Governor and Captain-General of Bahia in 1767 and, two years later, Viceroy of Brazil, a post which he held until 1779.

friends. Its soldiers were recruited among the poorest, simplest and most ignorant people, who could not avoid the countless existing exemptions from recruitment (which were still in force in 1757). The needs of personnel and training were forgotten. As the Marquis of Pombal later pointed out, the situation at the end of the reign of João V was aggravated by the King's illness: 'One of the sad effects which the severe infirmity of Dom João V necessarily caused in this kingdom throughout the eight years of its duration was the quasi-extinction of the troops'.[3]

A few rare measures taken at the beginning of the new reign did not change this situation. When it was necessary to move military forces to Lisbon after the earthquake of 1755, the regrettable state in which the army found itself was clearly demonstrated. 'This is why Sebastião de Carvalho reiterated his orders, so that the officers, who were largely absent from the regiments, might present themselves without delay and might remain there continuously, thus restoring their discipline and training their soldiers through frequent exercises. [...] So that, the legislator said, in all the provinces military ardour and regularity in the discipline, aptitude and cleanliness of the troops, might be reborn'.[4]

3 Lúcio de Azevedo, *O Marquez de Pombal*, pp. 285 ff.

4 Pombal, Appensos da contrariedade sobre o libello famoso, Appenso II, no. 37. Ms da Bibliotheca da Academia Real das Sciencias, transcribed in Latino Coelho, *História Política e Militar*, Vol.III, p.60n.

Under this precarious situation in the army, when it became clear that Portugal would most likely not be able to avoid getting caught up in the whirlwind of war, the need for the country to change this situation and find someone who knew how to organise and command the army turned into an urgency. This much-needed transformation required important political decisions in the context of the reconstruction of the military force whilst simultaneously obtaining British aid.

**Exercise of Command**

The state of the army was essentially due to lack of attention by the political power to the maintenance of a military force. There was, however, also another contributing factor: the lack of senior officers who were able to assert their authority by way of their competence, up-to-date knowledge and experience in recent campaigns. In the eighteenth century, senior military posts continued to be assigned to individuals who were obviously not qualified for their jobs.[5]

During the reign of João V, numerous foreign officers were admitted to the Portuguese army, particularly in the fields of artillery and engineering. While some possessed particular knowledge and experience, which was of relevance to a better performance, all of them lacked the national feeling that made the difference between trying to carry one's duty and serving one's country with love. Machiavelli had pointed out that mercenaries lacked any reason to die for the prince: this was the case with most of them here.

At the highest echelons of the army, few were highly qualified, except for rare and honourable exceptions. Unsurprisingly then, when Portugal's entry into the war became imminent, there was a need to obtain commanders from abroad. Above all, it was crucial to find someone recognizably competent who could organise and command the army. William, Count of Schaumburg-Lippe, the lord of a small state in Germany who had served with the allied army in Germany under British command, was invited and appointed Marshal-General to play this role. In the words of Latino Coelho, 'his coming to Portugal, although it was in a certain way a tarnish to the military genius of the Portuguese, can safely be commemorated as the beginning of our military reform and improvement'.[6]

'Wilhelm I, reigning Count of Schaumburg-Lippe, Generalissimo of the Army of His Majesty the King of Portugal and the Algarve, also Field Marshal of His Majesty the King of Great Britain, Knight of the Black Eagle Order of the Kingdom of Prussia'. (Engraving by C. W. Bock after a drawing by W. Strack)

5 Example of this abounded, such as 'the entrustment of a military command of a province to a bishop', the fact that 'the government of the fort of Peniche was entrusted in 1722 to the Count of Atouguia [...] while he was still an infant,' and the sale of 'the post [...] of artillery tenant [...] as an hereditary position in 1748, to an individual for the amount of 150 000 cruzados'; see Latino Coelho, *História Política e Militar*, Vol.III, p.49.

6 Latino Coelho, *História Política e Militar*, Vol.III, p.67.

The Marshal-General gained the King's confidence and the admiration and the friendship of Sebastião de Carvalho. This was facilitated by a number of reasons. One of them was the urgency of having a commander of high quality in the Portuguese Army, an aspect which the Count of Oeiras had understood as the war had kept approaching. Another was the urgent need to confront the enemy with national and auxiliary troops, and to provide organisation, discipline, morale, and effectiveness to the coming campaign. Furthermore, there was the fact that the Count of Oeiras had found the right man for this purpose in the Count of Lippe, and that the latter felt the political support he needed. This happy marriage between the political leadership and the military command would pay off, not only in the campaign but also in the reorganisation of the army that followed it for a number of years.

The Count of Lippe was born in London on 24 January 1724. He was, therefore, 36 years old when he commanded the Portuguese army and its British auxiliary corps. He studied during the years of 1740 and 1741 in Leiden in the Netherlands and in Montpellier in France, following philosophical, mathematical, and military courses. He entered very early in the service of the British Guards as a lieutenant, in which role, at the age of 19, he was present at the battle of Dettingen with his father, who was a general in the service of the Netherlands. He enlisted in the British navy in the following year of 1744, but quit it shortly after, for lack of health. He then participated in a new campaign in Italy at the orders of the Austrian general, his kinsman, the Count of Schulenburg, after which he interrupted his military life.

Portrait of the Count of Lippe in British uniform. Copy of a painting by Johann Georg Ziesenis of 1770, extant in the fortress of Wilhelmstein. (Military Museum, Lisbon)

He travelled again through Germany, Italy, and Hungary, and did it with prudent observation. As a result of this, as well as of his rule upon his people, a profound change took place in his mind and, according to his biographer, he transformed from a bold and feverish young man into a serious and thoughtful person, and a prudent and enlightened military leader. It was he who established obligatory military service in his country, calling for the participation of all the population in its defence, a means by which he protected it from the depredations that the French people carried in neighbouring from 1756 to 1763.

In the year of 1757 the count and the troops of his small state united with the Hanoverian army, of whose artillery he was appointed grand master by George II. In this capacity he took part in the battles of Crefeld, Minden, Lutherberg and Vellinghaussen; in the assaults on Munster, Cassel, Wesel, and Marburg; and in the withdrawal from Kampsen, which he was given the task of covering.[7]

## Portuguese Forces

It is not easy to accurately quantify the national personnel and military forces that existed in 1762. There were several reasons for this. Some units were dispersed throughout the garrisons of multiple settlements and forts. Others were diverted from the garrison settlements where they stationed to be used in the campaign. In the face of military threat, decrees called for the augmentation of the army. The consequent hasty recruitment, the lack of preparation of much of the personnel, and the displacement of many young men from their places of origin, led to a large number of desertions.

However, by using the careful analysis by Ernesto Pereira Sales and a few other documents, it is possible to conclude that there were 26 regiments, 23 of which originated in the army structure that had been defined in 1715 while the other three resulted from the splitting of the Regiments of Porto, Chaves and Bragança that occurred in April 1762.[8] In addition to these, there were also two battalions of Swiss troops, which were created on 27 June of the same year. Each regiment had two battalions, with a total establishment of 1,500 men. This means that, if the units had been complete, the overall strength of the Portuguese infantry would have amounted to around 40,000 men, approximately one third of whom were, however, dedicated to the defence of the forts and of those portions of the country that were not directly influenced by the campaign but which it was not possible to leave unprotected. In reality, however, according to the personnel chart of 26 September, there were only 1,454 officers and 13,248 soldiers in the infantry units (the infantry regiments having approximately 500 soldiers each; not enough for even one full-strength battalion).[9]

In terms of cavalry, there were 11 regiments, of which 10 had been set up in time of peace and one had been set up for this campaign (Regiment of Mecklenburg, named for its colonel who had accompanied the Count to Portugal – this regiment still existed in 2005, as a regiment of armoured vehicles, under the name Cavalry Regiment No.4 ). The total number of cavalry personnel was 4,500 men and the units, it may be affirmed, were complete. In the official chart of 26 September, 479 officers and 3,998 soldiers are indicated, very close to the establishment strength.[10]

7 Gen. Augusto Xavier Palmeirim, *Alguns Factos Militares Portuguezes do Século XVIII* (Lisboa: Tipografia Universal, 1873), pp 8-9.

8 Ernesto Pereira Sales tried to survey the Portuguese units and quantify their personnel: see Ernesto Augusto Pereira Sales, *O Conde de Lippe em Portugal* (Vila Nova de Famalicão: Grandes ateliers gráficos "Minerva", de G. Pinto de Sousa & Irmão, 1936), which provides the background for this section. Much like nowadays, the northern part of the country, which was more densely populated, supplied the largest numbers in personnel, to the extent that in some cities the regiments were split.

9 A.H.M., DIV3/8/1/24, Mapa de efectivos, em 26 de Setembro de 1762.

10 A.H.M., DIV3/8/1/24, Mapa de efectivos, em 26 de Setembro de 1762.

There was also a Regiment of Royal Volunteers, that was half-infantry and half-cavalry, but it was formed by drawing on men from the existing regiments, under an order by Lippe dated 8 August 1762.

In terms of artillery, there were two regiments, the Artillery Regiment of the Court and the Artillery Regiment of Alentejo, both being constituted by two battalions. The total number of artillery personnel was about 3,000 men, and in August 1762 they held 47 guns of various calibres. These guns and their respective ammunition and subunits were assigned in support of the main bodies in the order of battle, according to the circumstances.

As indicated, the personnel on the ranks were far less than they should organically have been:

> When the Spanish entered Portugal, our regiments lacked both officers and soldiers; to complete the troops, batches of recruits were hastily and violently set up and these were included in the units that were already encamped in Tomar and in bordering settlements [...] However, in the general muster of 7 August only eighteen infantry battalions and four cavalry regiments, together with some artillery forces, appeared, all out of a total of five thousand five hundred and eighty-two men.[11]

This number proves that many units were deprived of personnel, which lends support to the Count of Lippe's point of view, when he said that 'since it was necessary to leave a body in the North of the kingdom, because of the Spanish troops that were in Galicia, and it was also necessary to leave garrisons at the most exposed spots, all that was left to oppose that powerful army of the enemy was not more than 14 or 15,000 men at most, including the British troops'.[12]

The same idea about the shortage of personnel is contained in a letter dated 19 September from the Count of Lippe to the Count of Oeiras. Its author stated that he was 'mortified of being obliged to tell you that I do not yet find that there has been any significant change with respect to its quantity; It is true that recruits arrive every day, but this serves no purpose other than counterbalancing the number of those who desert, so much so that the total is almost always the same'.[13]

Although the cavalry was not short of personnel, as mentioned above, on 23 August Lippe complained about the 'extreme weakness' of the cavalry and insisted on the arrival of the Regiment of Mecklenburg. In his letter of 19 September, the Count kept on saying that 'the cavalry of our army is in a truly deplorable state'. However, he failed to clarify whether this was due to a shortage of personnel, horses or armament; only saying that it lacked a command. For this position, he proposed the Marquis of Marialva, by saying:

11 Pereira Sales, *O Conde de Lippe*, p.58.

12 Conde de Schaumbourg-Lippe, 'Memória sobre a Campanha de 1762', *Revista Militar*, 1849, p.183.

13 Anon. 'Carta do Conde de Lippe para o Conde de Oeiras, de 19 de Setembro', *Boletim do Arquivo Histórico Militar*, 1934, p.267. The original documents of the correspondence between the Count of Lippe and the Count of Oeiras are extant at the Military Historical Archive.

Friedrich Wilhelm Ernst, reigning count of Schaumburg-Lippe (1724-1777), was born in London and was an illegitimate grandson of George I of Great Britain. Considered the great artillery expert of his time, he was appointed as artillery general for the Army of Hannover, a German possession of the kings of Great Britain, in 1756. During the Seven Years War, before coming to Portugal, he participated in the battles of Hastenbeck, Lutterburg and Minden and commanded the sieges of Wesel and Kassel. (Military Museum, Lisbon)

'View of the scaffold as it was seen on the Belém square on 13 January 1759'. Colour engraving showing the execution, decided by the Court of High Treason, of the Duke of Aveiro, the Marquis of Távora and his relatives. An infantry force with its flags can be seen on the first row. (City Museum, Lisbon)

Sketches of an officer, a soldier and a drummer of the Second Infantry Regiment of Chaves. The second regiment was set up as the result of a decision to divide the Infantry Regiment of Chaves into two and was commanded by a recently promoted colonel, Francisco José de Morais Pimentel. For the uniforms of the unit, cloth from Zaragoza was used, much as happened with many of the new regiments. The growth in the number of soldiers of the battalions from 360, as regulated in 1734, to 770 by April 1762 generated an enormous problem in the production of uniforms which could not be solved if the uniforms maintained their uniform characteristics. (Sketches from the Album *Mapa do Fardamento que por ordem de S. Mag, Se fes na Cidade do Porto debaixo da inspecção do Tenente Gn.al João de Almada*, Military Historical Archives, Lisbon)

A brother of the future Marquis of Pombal, Francisco Xavier de Mendonça Furtado (1701-1769) was appointed Governor and Captain-General of the recently created Captainship of Grão-Pará e Maranhão in 1751, a post which he carried out until 1759. On this year, he was appointed Joint Secretary of State of the Kingdom's Affairs. In 1762 he was appointed to the position of Secretary of State of the Overseas Domains and of the Navy. As an army officer, he is shown here wearing the uniform of a lieutenant-general. (Unsigned and undated painting, private collection)

1
2
3
4
5
RIO TEJO

## The Campaign in Beira Baixa and Alto Alentejo: Operations from 14 September to 15 November 1762.

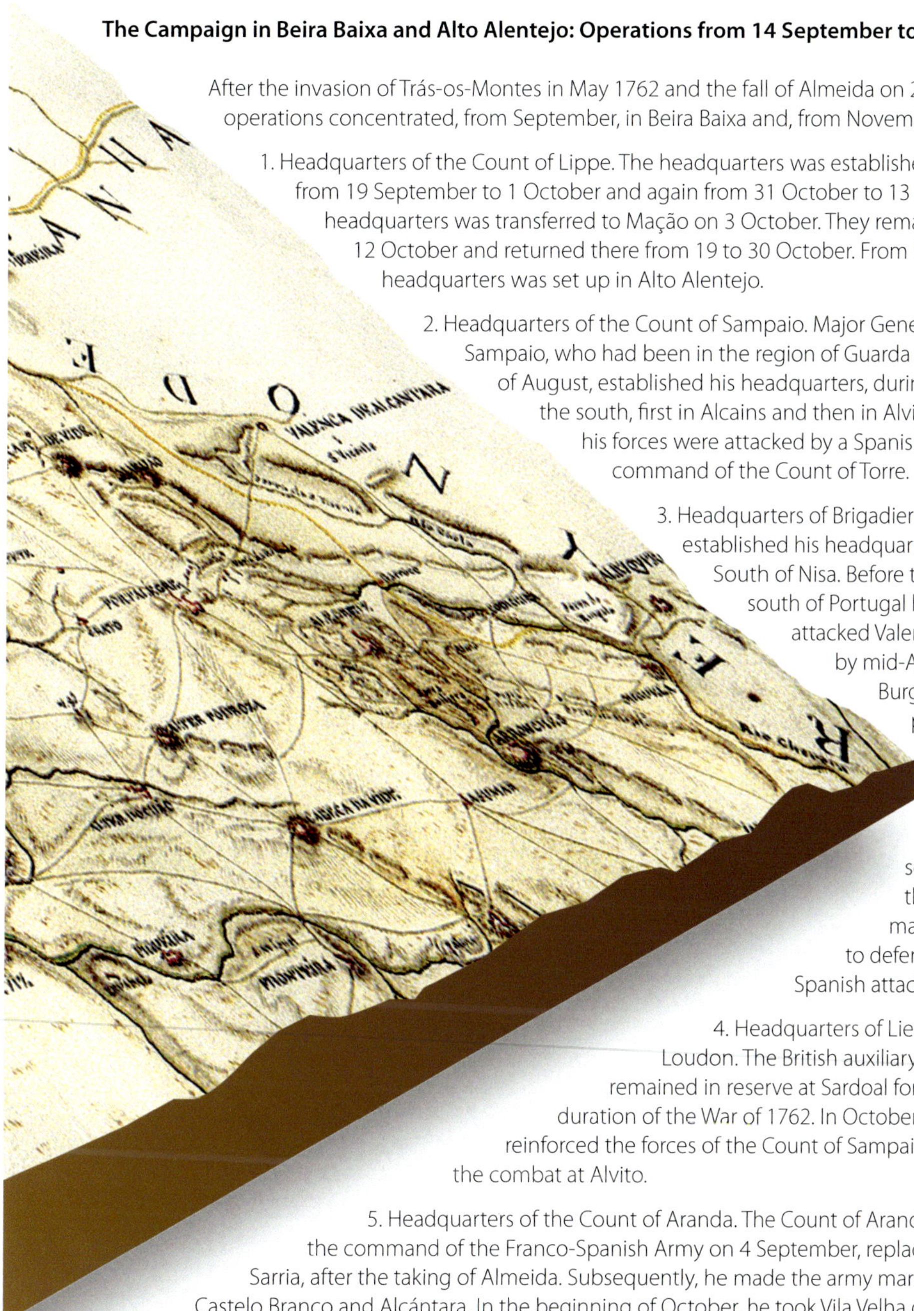

After the invasion of Trás-os-Montes in May 1762 and the fall of Almeida on 25 August, military operations concentrated, from September, in Beira Baixa and, from November, in Alto Alentejo.

1. Headquarters of the Count of Lippe. The headquarters was established in Abrantes from 19 September to 1 October and again from 31 October to 13 November. The headquarters was transferred to Mação on 3 October. They remained there until 12 October and returned there from 19 to 30 October. From 14 November the headquarters was set up in Alto Alentejo.

2. Headquarters of the Count of Sampaio. Major General the Count of Sampaio, who had been in the region of Guarda during the month of August, established his headquarters, during the campaign in the south, first in Alcains and then in Alvito. On 3 October, his forces were attacked by a Spanish unit under the command of the Count of Torre.

3. Headquarters of Brigadier Burgoyne. Burgoyne established his headquarters in Tolosa, to the South of Nisa. Before the campaign in the south of Portugal began, Burgoyne attacked Valencia de Alcántara by mid-August. In October, Burgoyne was unable to prevent the fall of Vila Velha do Ródão, but he stopped the Spanish army in its advance southwards, towards the Alto Alentejo and managed in November to defend the province from Spanish attacks.

4. Headquarters of Lieutenant General Loudon. The British auxiliary infantry forces remained in reserve at Sardoal for most of the duration of the War of 1762. In October, two battalions reinforced the forces of the Count of Sampaio and participated in the combat at Alvito.

5. Headquarters of the Count of Aranda. The Count of Aranda took charge of the command of the Franco-Spanish Army on 4 September, replacing the Marquis of Sarria, after the taking of Almeida. Subsequently, he made the army march South towards Castelo Branco and Alcántara. In the beginning of October, he took Vila Velha do Ródão and tried later to march towards Abrantes. Having been defeated, he withdrew to Spain and tried to attack several settlements in the Alto Alentejo from 8 to 15 November. He was again unsuccessful and on 22 November requested a suspension of the conflict.

Soldier of the Infantry Regiment of Viana, which stood under the command of Colonel Sebastião Pinto Roby. The Infantry Regiment of Viana was one of the few regiments that were not divided into several units during the War of 1762. The uniform of the Portuguese Army, until 1763, was white with colour enhancements. (*Mapa do Fardamento que por ordem de S. Mag, Se fes na Cidade do Porto debaixo da inspecção do Tenente Gn.al João de Almada*, Military Historical Archives, Lisbon)

Drummer of the Second Infantry Regiment of Porto. (*Mapa do Fardamento que por ordem de S. Mag, Se fes na Cidade do Porto debaixo da inspecção do Tenente Gn.al João de Almada*, Military Historical Archives, Lisbon)

An Officer from the Infantry Regiment of Porto, which was under the command of Jorge Francisco Machado de Mendonça. The uniforms of the two Infantry Regiments of Porto were green. (*Mapa do Fardamento que por ordem de S. Mag, Se fes na Cidade do Porto debaixo da inspecção do Tenente Gn.al João de Almada*, Military Historical Archives, Lisbon)

A Soldier from the Infantry Regiment of Porto. The regiment originated from the Tercio of the Porto Townhall, which was created in 1659. (*Mapa do Fardamento que por ordem de S. Mag, Se fes na Cidade do Porto debaixo da inspecção do Tenente Gn.al João de Almada*, Military Historical Archives, Lisbon)

Portuguese Auxiliary Cavalry. Sketch of an officer and a soldier from the Companhias de Éguas of Beira. (*Mapa do Fardamento que por ordem de S. Mag, Se fes na Cidade do Porto debaixo da inspecção do Tenente Gn.al João de Almada,* Military Historical Archives, Lisbon)

'... I take it that, since this nobleman has made a particular study of many types of knowledge that are necessary to a cavalry officer, this body which is so useful would immediately arise from its current state'.[14]

In addition to its regular army, Portugal also had about 25,000 men, either auxiliaries or of the *Ordenança*, who could be employed in various functions, including for the garrison of forts. *Ordenanças*, under this name or another and usually organised in units with identical names to those of the regular units, had a long tradition in Portugal. They had been created under the precocious idea that military duty should be compulsory and universal (this concept would only be fully put into practice under the conscription system that emerged out of the French Revolution). They can be seen from the period of foundation of the Portuguese nation, in the *fossado* and *apelido* duties, to which the populations were subject; in the military obligations that were attached to the councils and were included in the *foral* documents of the early Kings of Portugal; and in the establishment of the military duties that were laid down in the *Ordenações Sebásticas*, the sixteenth-century laws of King Sebastião, and were later recovered during the Portuguese Restoration of Independence.

The creation of these forces during the period of the Restoration was accepted without reluctance, in contrast to what had happened during the reign of King Sebastião, at which point the setting up of similar forces had sparked popular reaction.[15] This was certainly a consequence of widespread awareness that it was necessary to undergo sacrifices in the context of the war with Spain. In 1709, the Law for Second-Line Troops (*Regimento das Ordenanças*) of King Sebastião, a decree that regulated the territorial troops and the forms of military backup, was reinstated, allowing for the existence of what one might call a second line of defence. However, because for many years military threat was not obvious, concerns about its efficiency shrank and became heavily dependent on the dedication of their commanders and the support of the regional authorities.

In the *Guerra Fantástica*, this militia came to show some of its virtues and flaws. This can be seen, on the one hand, in the difficulties which it created to the enemy in Trás-os-Montes region, and, on the other, in the weak combat value that they demonstrated in defending forts. Reflecting on their performance, the Count of Lippe would later comment in a letter of 1764 to the Count of Oeiras that 'in order to take advantage of the militia, which is called to help, it is necessary to keep it well armed, controlled and in shape [...]. I do not dare, however, to advocate its suppression, unless it can be replaced by something better, [but] I think that six or eight thousand good infantry men, that is, the fifth or seventh part of the number of auxiliaries, would render a much safer service in time of war'.[16]

14 Anon. 'Carta do Conde de Lippe para o Conde de Oeiras, de 19 de Setembro', p.267

15 Gen. Ferreira Martins, *História do Exército Português* (Lisboa: Inquérito, 1945), p.144.

16 Barrento, 'O Exército Português Antes e Depois do Conde de Lippe', p.283.

## Foreign Auxiliary Forces

Following London's positive response to a request of forces from Portugal, British reinforcements began to arrive on 6 May. This was a force of 7-8,000 men, which was organised into six infantry regiments, one cavalry regiment (dragoons), and eight artillery companies. These units gradually arrived in Portugal and reorganised for the campaign, and only marched towards the advanced camp near Abrantes in August. The force's command was to be assigned to General Lord Tyrawley. He was 72 years old, had been a representative of Great Britain in the Portuguese Court and had handled the issue of the arrival of the British auxiliary forces with the Portuguese Government. However, as George III had placed the British force under the command of the Count of Lippe, who was a much younger officer than Lord Tyrawley, the latter asked London to withdraw and return to his country. The direct command of the British forces was then assigned to Lieutenant General Lord Loudoun.

In addition to the British units, the Portuguese forces were also reinforced with foreign personnel, who accompanied the Count of Lippe on his trip to Portugal, or who offered themselves individually to serve the Portuguese Army. Their presence was particularly important because of Portugal's lack of officers with command and war experience. Three British officers – Townshend, Carey, and Craufurd – were made Portuguese lieutenant generals, and three more – Lennox, Fraser, and Clerk – were made major

Composition showing the British brigade commanded by Major-General Kingley, made up of the 20th, 25th, and 51st Foot fighting back against a charge by the French cavalry during the Battle of Minden, 1 August 1759. (Watercolour by Harry Payne)

generals; several infantry colonels were assigned to command Portuguese regiments, two cavalry colonels also commanded Portuguese regiments, and several infantry and artillery lower-echelon officers were also seconded to the Portuguese service.

Aide-de-Camp to King George II in 1743, John Campbell, Lord Loudon (1705-1782) was appointed Captain-General and Governor of the British colony of Virginia in February 1756. In March, he was appointed Commander-in-Chief of the British forces in North America, but in 1757 he was summoned to England due to the Louisburg setback. He was appointed commander of the British forces in Portugal in 1762 but his performance was unremarkable (Fictional engraving that was included in the manuscript *Notícias dos Sucessos da Guerra de Hespanha*… (News on the developments in the Spanish War…), belonging to the Library of the Military Academy, Lisbon, doc. 2058, p. 245)

## Enemy Forces

For some of the same reasons given when referring to national forces, it is also difficult to accurately describe the personnel and the forces which the Franco-Spanish Army committed to the *Guerra Fantástica*. Some units did not leave Spain but were nevertheless involved in the war; supplies of personnel were sent to the Spanish border forts; the army placed garrisons in some of the Portuguese forts that were conquered and thus shifted to its control, which meant that these forces became unavailable for participation in battles elsewhere. The proximity of the area of operations to the border facilitated the movement of the units to both sides.

In 1760, before the intervention in Portugal, the Spanish army had, in total, 43 infantry regiments, 12 of which were made up of foreigners – Walloons, Italians, Irish and Swiss – 20 cavalry regiments and 10 of dragoons, and various artillery and engineering units.[17] The infantry regiments were made up of two battalions, with a nominal 600 men each, organised into 11 companies of musketeers and one of grenadiers. The cavalry regiments had about 300 men apiece. As was the case in Portugal, the general and senior officers belonged to the nobility.

As for the Spanish forces that intervened in Portugal, in December 1761 Carlos III referred to a total number, when he ordered the artillery commander, Lieutenant General Count of Gazola, to assemble and organise the artillery to support the army of 30,000 men that would be invading Portugal.[18] When, at the end of the year, the Count of Gazola detailed the artillery needed to support the force, he counted 94 guns and mortars of

17 According to A.H.M.-DIV/1/7/1/11, *Opérations de l'Armée d'Espagne selon les Messieurs de La Haye*, there were '64 battalions, and 45 full squadrons that were in very good shape', of which, under the orders of Sarriá, 36 battalions, 35 squadrons, four artillery battalions and two communication battalions, with nine lieutenant generals; in Galicia, eight battalions, six battalions of militia and two squadrons; and, in Andalucia, four battalions, four battalions of militia and eight squadrons.

18 António Maria Mourinho, 'Invasão de Trás-os-Montes e das Beiras na Guerra dos Sete Anos pelos Exércitos Bourbónicos, em 1762, através da Correspondência Oficial dos Comandantes-Chefes Marquês de Sarriá e Conde de Aranda…' (paper presented at the Academy of History, on 22 April 1983), *Anais da Academia Portuguesa*, II Série. Volume 31, 1986, p.380.

Types of Spanish soldiers of the second half of the eighteenth century.

various calibres, to be used on several occasions, especially for the siege of Almeida and for the attempt to cross the Tagus at Vila Velha de Ródão. However, this same artillery caused great difficulties to the movements of the army when the campaigning in very rugged areas, along bad roads, and under unfavourable atmospheric conditions, as was the case in the botched attempts to march from Chaves and Vila Real to Porto and, later, to advance from the region of Castelo Branco to Tomar and Abrantes.

On 12 June, after the invasion of Trás-os-Montes, 12 French battalions, under the command of Lieutenant General de Beauvau, united with the Spanish Army, with a total of approximately 10,000 men.[19]

19 Mourinho, 'Invasão de Trás-os-Montes e das Beiras', p.395.

6

# Fantastical War

The Spanish Ambassador in Lisbon left on 27 April but stayed in Estremoz, where awaited the departure of the Portuguese Ambassador in Madrid, Dom José da Silva, which only took place on 4 May.[1] Following the withdrawal of the ambassadors, a sign that diplomacy had failed to prevent war, the invasion of Portugal began with an army of about 30,000 men under the command of the Lieutenant General and commander-in-chief Don Nicolás de Carvajal y Lancaster Vivero Noroña de Sande Padilla y Montezuma, Marquis of Sarriá.

## Initial Actions in Trás-os-Montes

On 24 February 1762, Carlos III ordered the Marquis of Sarriá to enter Portugal, but the forces were not yet ready for action and only on 2 March did the Spanish commander-in-chief establish his headquarters in Salamanca. On 16 March, the King signed the plan of operations, which envisaged that the invasion would take place on the Portuguese north-eastern border, between Puebla de Sanabria and Ciudad Rodrigo. An exchange of correspondence between the King and Sarriá followed. This exchange reveals Carlos III's impatience to carry out the invasion, which collided with local reasons that rendered it impossible to cross the River Esla, a tributary on the right bank of the Douro, which carried an abundant flow of water due to high rainfall and the thawing of snows on the hills of Leon, Astorga and Sanabria.[2]

At the end of March, the King continued to insist that action be taken, but only at the end of April did the force seem to be prepared. On 29 April, the Marquis informed the Court in Madrid that he would be initiating military manoeuvres and would be taking the fort of Miranda do Douro. Sarriá left Zamora on 1 May and, marching in three columns, he advanced towards Alcañices, where he camped on 4 May. The following day, a significant part of the forces entered Portuguese territory.

Sarriá still tried to avoid armed conflict, by having a proclamation affixed in various places of the North of Portugal on 30 April. This proclamation read that the Spanish Army 'does not aim to make the war at them', that no Portuguese individual would be treated badly, and that it would only ask the people 'to attend with food, and any other aid that the army needed, with

Trás-os-Montes. Map of the province, published in the work by João Baptista de Castro, *Mappa de Portugal antigo e moderno, tomo I*, in 1762.

The Douro at Miranda do Douro.

the certainty that they would be paid for that'. This proclamation and the invasion of Trás-os-Montes gave rise to a Royal Decree on the Portuguese side, which explained that France and Spain wished to dispose of 'these kingdoms as if they were their own, so as to invade, occupy and usurp, under the incompatible pretext of assisting him against enemies', and that they were 'invading, at the same time, with an army, divided into different bodies, my provinces, and attacking my forts'. On this basis, the Royal Decree determined that 'I have thus made known to all my vassals that they consider the violators of the independent sovereignty of my crown and invaders of my kingdom as publicly declared aggressors and enemies'.[3]

It is hard to understand what the enemy forces wanted to achieve by invading that province when they started their operations in Portugal. Did they want to test the will of the Portuguese to defend themselves? Did they want to convert the threat of invasion into reality, in order to force the Portuguese monarch to join the Family Compact? Did they intend to conquer Porto and deny it to the British, in order to achieve a change in the Portuguese position, and then, should this not occur, to march on Lisbon? Or did they just wish to occupy a part of the country? We do not know for sure what the intent may have been that led to choosing this plan, but some clues exist and it is possible, on the basis of these, to put forward a few interpretations.

For Lúcio de Azevedo, the idea of the French Cabinet was to march directly upon Lisbon, which, according to Choiseul, 'would have had an immense effect if the Spaniards had known how to put it into practice'.[4] Nonetheless, Carlos III, wishing to keep his sister away from the war, decided to try to seize Porto, instead of sending the army over to Lisbon by way of Almeida. However, as the army entered through Trás-os-Montes, he was forced to change the base of the operations from Ciudad Rodrigo to Zamora. Lúcio de Azevedo has also suggested that it may have been considered that, if the enemy forces conquered a part of Portugal, they would be able to obtain 'valuable compensations' from Britain at the end of the war.[5]

The argument to spare the queen is also supported in the *História de España*, which mentions that Carlos III, wishing Mariana Victoria, his sister and wife of José I, 'not to be forced to closely witness the horrors of fighting', accepted a plan of operations by the Catalan engineer Gabert, according to which the Marquis of Sarriá 'was to occupy the Provinces of Trás-Os-Montes and Entre Duero e Miño [sic] and to become the owner of Porto'.[6]

The Count of Lippe interpreted the decision to attack the northern part of the country as linked to the weak military dispositive in that province, which could grant the attacker great freedom of action. For him, it appeared 'that the purpose of his invasion in Traz-os-Montes had been to recognise this

3 The Proclamation and the Royal Decree are fully transcribed in Luz Soriano, *História do Reinado de El-Rei D. José*, Vol.I, pp.483-484.

4 In Memoirs of the Duke of Choiseul, p.338, quoted in Lúcio de Azevedo, *O Marquez de Pombal*, p.282.

5 Lúcio de Azevedo, *O Marquez de Pombal*, p.283.

6 Anon., *História de España*, p.84.

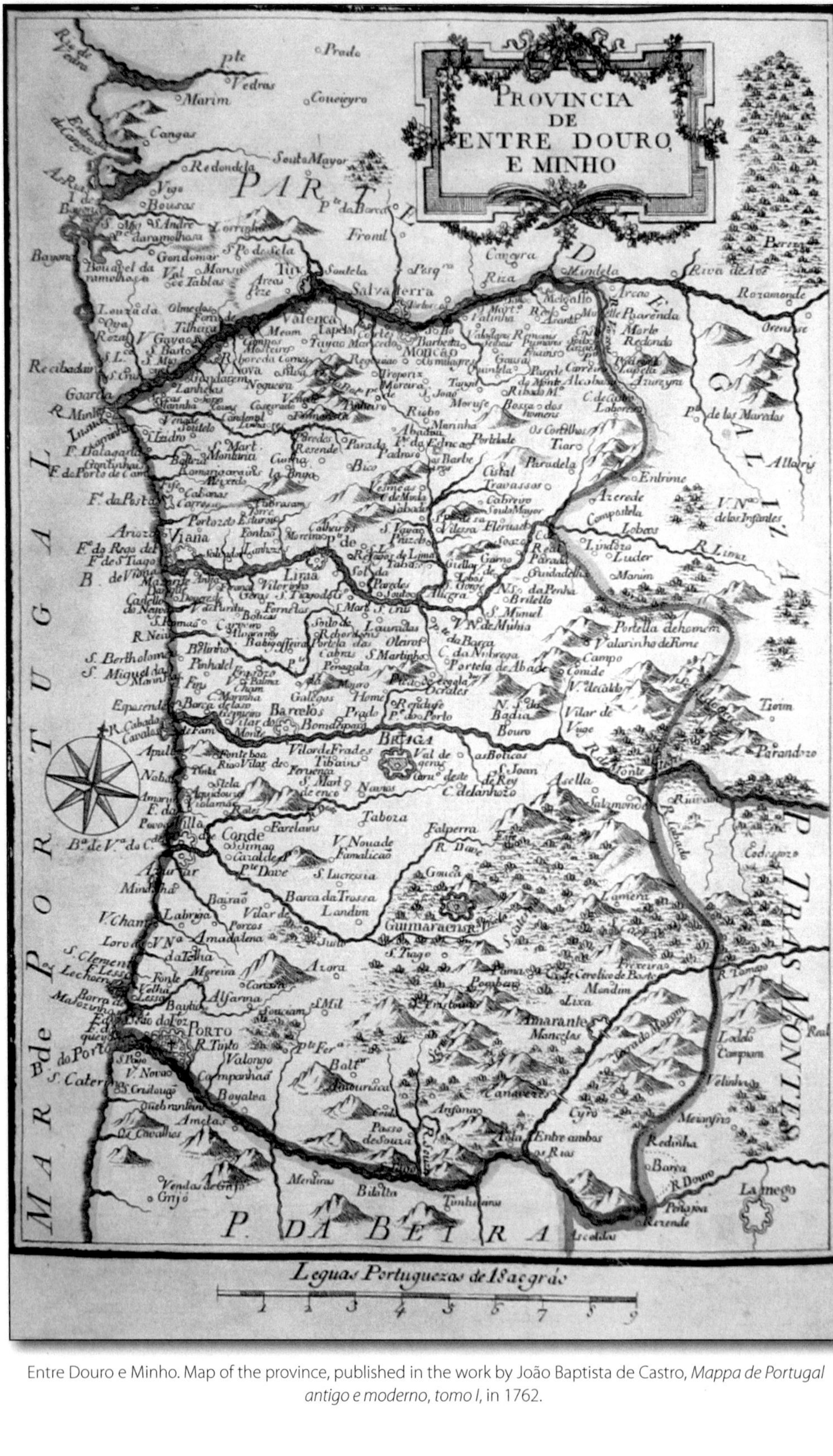


Entre Douro e Minho. Map of the province, published in the work by João Baptista de Castro, *Mappa de Portugal antigo e moderno, tomo I*, in 1762.

province and the banks of the Douro', in order, on crossing it, 'to infiltrate [the province of] Beira Baixa as was his intention'.[7] António Mourinho, partly corroborates this idea of the Count when he says: 'eight days after the fall of Miranda do Douro, [Sarriá] announces on the 13th [of May] that he plans to attack Moncorvo and cross the Douro, so as to attack the Portuguese troops in Abrantes'.[8]

On 3 May, Colonel Alexandro O'Reylli, commander of a light force forming the vangaurd of the Spanish Army, crossed the Portuguese border between Senhora da Luz and Constantin. He then moved on to Duas Igrejas and proceeded to Bemposta, by way of Sendim and Urrós, to survey the terrain and avoid the withdrawal or the reinforcement of the garrison of Miranda do Douro. After that, he returned north, via Picote, up to Miranda, and during the journey he conducted a reconnaissance of that stretch of the right bank of the Douro.

The force intended to conquer Miranda entered Portuguese territory on 5 May, via Constantin, and occupied Ifanes, Póvoa, Malhadas and Duas Igrejas, putting itself in position to surround the fort. The backup forces, which were initially in Spanish territory, later went to occupy the region of Constantin. The Marquis de Sarriá left Alcañices on 4 May and installed his headquarters in the region of Duas Igrejas, where he remained during the occupation of Trás-os-Montes, which lasted for about two months.

Miranda fort was the first target of the Spanish Army, possibly because it was considered that it would be difficult to keep on with operations in the province of Trás-os-Montes without neutralizing the place. Its garrison was made up of the 2nd Regiment of Infantry of Bragança, an artillery detachment, two engineering detachments, a company of grenadiers, a company of riflemen, four companies of auxiliary troops and a cavalry detachment. Colonel Bento José de Figueiredo Sarmento was governor of the fort.

On 4 May, the Governor of Miranda do Douro, after having been notified to accept the Spanish Army on friendly terms, sent Major General Luis Xavier da Veiga to the border of Constantin with the following reply: 'he had no orders either from his King or from his superiors to let foreign troops be in Portuguese territory and would treat those who were so as enemies and would defend the Fort to the last drop of blood'.[9]

On May 8, the fort's artillery opened fire on O'Reylli's forces, with '14 cannon shots',[10] but at approximately 7 o'clock in the afternoon a strong explosion broke out inside the fortification. The burst happened in the gunpowder magazine, which was estimated to contain about 20 tons of gunpowder.[11] The blast opened two breaches in the wall, one to the east and the other to the west, and an estimated 400 people were killed, including

7 Schaumbourg-Lippe, 'Memória sobre a Campanha de 1762', *Revista Militar*, 1849, pp.182 ff.

8 Mourinho, *Guerra do Mirandum*, p.24.

9 Mourinho, *Invasão de Trás-os-Montes e das Beiras*, p.387.

10 Report by the Marquis of Sarriá, of 12 May, General Archive of Simancas, in Mourinho, *Guerra do Mirandum*, p.15.

11 Despite the high degree of damage which the explosion produced, which indicates that it involved a significant quantity of explosive, the reference to 20 tons seems exaggerated. Later

soldiers and civilians. Sarriá himself wrote to Madrid that 'we see that many relatives are crying; inside the fort cries are continuous and the faces breathe anguish, estimates of the damage being that around five hundred people were lost.'[12] Some people said that the explosion of the magazine had occurred 'by chance or by treason.'[13] However, given the number of dead, the damage, the report of Sarriá to the King and the actions of the Governor, there seems to be no ground to suspect treason, and this must have been a case of negligence in dealing with a sensitive substance such as is gunpowder.[14]

The Fort governor sent a letter to Sarriá requesting a three-day truce to bury the dead and treat the wounded, but this request was denied. On 9 May, the Governor surrendered and troops under Lieutenant General Riva Agüerro entered the city and occupied the fort.

After the occupation of Miranda do Douro, the light forces of O'Reylli marched on Vimioso and Outeiro and, on May 12, troops under Marquis of Ceballos, who had left Alcañices, encamped in Gimonde, where they received notice of the surrender of Bragança, which was soon occupied by the O'Reylli units. After the fall of Miranda do Douro, Bragança would have been unable to resist.

After Bragança was occupied, O'Reylli advanced on Chaves, which surrendered without resistance on 21 May. Meanwhile, the Marquis of Castremañes, with around 2,000 men, marched on Torre de Moncorvo, which surrendered, also unopposed, on 23 May. On that same day, O'Reylli's units arrived in Vila Real, where O'Reylli began to notice a lot of animosity on the part of the countrymen, many of them having been seen armed on the surrounding hills. On 1 June, O'Reylli, fearing a popular revolt, returned to Chaves.

Despite these easy initial successes of the invading army, the attempts to cross the Douro, as well as efforts to progress to the west, were botched, and the insurrectionary environment increased in intensity. In addition to the difficulties of the terrain and the precariousness of the routes for movements by the artillery, the Spanish forces encountered resistance from militias and popular groups, all of which suggested that the manoeuvres of the invading army on national territory would not be carried out without a cost.

On 24 May, the forces of the Marquis of Castremañes attempted to cross the Douro at Vila Nova de Foz Côa, but the boats had been rendered inoperative and, on the south bank, an armed 'crowd of people' belonging to the militia and acting under the command of the British Lieutenant Colonel O'Hara forced him to return to Torre de Moncorvo. The attempts that were made

---

during the year, 40 tons were stored in Estremoz, as support for the whole army in the province of Alentejo.

12 Report by the Marquis of Sarriá, of 12 May, General Archive of Simancas, in Mourinho, *Guerra do Mirandum*, pp.15-18.

13 Luz Soriano, *História do Reinado de El-Rei D. José*, Vol.I, p.489.

14 This suspicion was raised as early as in 1763 in *Notícias dos Sucessos da Guerra de Espanha e França contra Portugal no Ano de 1762*, in which its author accused the Governor of the Fort. Given the degree of passion that pervades the document, it should be read with reservations. There is a copy of this document (Ref. B.E.E., 2058-b-18) at the Military Historical Archive: A.H.M.-DIV/1/7/5/19.

to advance towards Porto were not successful either. A body of 4,000 men, aiming to reach Braga via Montalegre, encountered not only geographical difficulties in their progress through the mountains, but also resistance from militiamen. The efforts made to penetrate Portuguese territory further south, via Vila Pouca de Aguiar and through the Marão hills, were also unfruitful. The passageways were defended by regular forces and by militias.

The next attempt to cross the Douro at Vila Nova de Foz Côa, where the Spanish army gathered a very high number of men, possibly 8-11,000, were also futile. In addition to these difficulties, rumours also spread that the Marquis of Marialva and Major Generals the Count of Angeja, Count of Arcos and José Leite de Sousa were approaching Lamego with seven regiments, British forces and militias. If this force were to enter Trás-os-Montes, it could divide the two wings of the Spanish Army, one of which was trying to reach Porto through the mountains while the other one was trying to cross the Douro onto its left bank. This was a very high risk for the invaders.[15]

Probably because of this environment, on 6 June, Carlos III gave up on the idea of conquering Porto, whilst ordering that the occupation of Chaves be consolidated. However, because the action of the armed civilians was increasing, with insistent attacks on the columns involved in logistics, Carlos III did not hide his displeasure and showed it to Sarriá. These actions upon these columns were so disruptive that they even forced the occupying army in the region of Chaves to reroute its resupplying channel via Puebla of Sanabria, as a way to avoid displacements within Portuguese territory.[16]

As a result of all the troubles found in trying to advance towards Porto and the left bank of the Douro, of the logistical problems raised by the guerrillas, and of the armed resistance and the fact that the terrain favoured defence and the action of irregular forces, the Spanish Army changed its plan. It withdrew its forces (the bulk of them encamped at Duas Igrejas on 29 June) via Alcañices and left only a garrison, formed of troops from Galicia, at the fort of Chaves.

Given the relative detachment of the theatre of operations from the aim of preventing the continuation of the Portuguese policy of connection to Britain, the action of the Spanish in Trás-os-Montes seems to have been only an attack of limited purpose, perhaps meant to be used as a useful bargaining chip in future conversations or as a manifestation of force in order to break the will of the Portuguese to resist. In any case, this action ran up against a clear opposition from the political leadership and the determination of the people, and only the fort of Chaves remained occupied. The remaining forces returned to Spain, as noted, to concentrate their efforts on the region surrounding Ciudad Rodrigo.

15 A.H.M.-DIV/1/7/1/11, Opérations de l'Armée d'Espagne selon les Messieurs de La Haye, and 1/7/1/24, Atestado sobre a Defesa da Passagem do Douro.

16 Mourinho, *Invasão de Trás-os-Montes e das Beiras*, p.394.

## Effort in Beira Alta

While the Spanish columns were operating in Trás-os-Montes, the reinforcements that had been requested from Britain began to arrive in Portugal. The British auxiliary force was important, given the state of weakness in which the Portuguese Army found itself, and also its symbolic value as an unequivocal demonstration of Britain's support. It included approximately 7,500 men and was made up of six infantry regiments, one cavalry regiment and one artillery detachment. The cavalry regiment was the 16th Light Dragoons, under Brigadier John Burgoyne whose actions during the campaign were often very important. Throughout the campaign the British auxiliary force was under the command of Lieutenant General Lord Loudoun, although some of its units were sometimes detached to other corps.

On 2 June, the Count of Schaumburg-Lippe landed in Lisbon, to be invested by Royal Decree as Marshal-General and Commander of the Portuguese Army on the following day. George III had also entrusted him with the post of Commander-in-Chief of the British forces that were stationed in Portugal. The Count immediately developed, in coordination with the political power, a continuous and dynamic programme of reorganisation of the Portuguese Army. In carrying it out, he chose, in his words, 'a camp between Abrantes and Rio Zezere, in which I hope I will gather, in the first days of August, nine Portuguese Infantry Regiments, four Cavalry Regiments, and one part of the Ammunition Depot'.[17]

While several units were concentrating in the regions of Tomar, Tancos, Torres Novas and other neighbouring settlements, the Count of Lippe went on an intense schedule of visits, in order to find out the state of the Army and, on 22 July, he established his headquarters in Abrantes.

The Count of Lippe was described in the following terms:

> He was very devoted to mathematical studies, to the military sciences, and especially to the artillery. He cultivated history, philosophy, literature, and the political sciences, while he was not a host in the field of medicine. He was familiar with the German, British, French, Italian, and Portuguese languages.
>
> He was well-versed in Latin, admired its classics, and above all explained Cesar's campaigns. He was very much an amateur of music and played the harpsichord masterfully. He drew perfectly, was strong in fencing, and rode wonderfully. He was endowed with a very fortunate physical constitution, was sober in food, and did not sleep much. He was so agile that he easily jumped over any obstacle five and a half feet high.
>
> He was of a more than regular stature, lean, nervous, and sturdy. His forehead was wide and prominent; eyes pierced, penetrating, and such as to inculcate majesty and empire, and right away an intelligent, benevolent spirit; aquiline nose, and a very small mouth. Ha was respectable altogether, sober in words,

17 Anon. 'Carta do Conde de Lippe para o Conde de Oeiras, de 19 de Setembro', p.247.

Portrait of the Count of Lippe; drawing attributed to Cavaleiro Faria (in *Notícias dos Sucessos da Guerra de Hespanha…* (News on the developments in the Spanish War…), manuscript of the Library of the Military Academy, Lisbon, doc. 2058)

> but these were always lucid and affable. Schmaltz qualifies him as a man full of peaceful grandeur.
>
> He wore a simple blue suit that was always buttoned, distinguishing himself only by the cross of the black eagle that was embroidered on his jacket. He always wore a cocked hat and high boots.[18]

After the forces that had invaded Trás-os-Montes had returned to Spain, the bulk of the Spanish Army gathered, as of 15 July, in the region of Ciudad Rodrigo. The French forces joined, as France had formally declared war on Portugal on 20 June.[19] The concentration of troops in this region clearly shows that Sarriá's suggestion, of 11 June, to attack Almeida had been approved and that there had been a change in the plan to invade Portuguese territory.[20] It was the Beira region that was now directly under threat. The enemy's army

18 Palmeirim, *Alguns Factos Militares Portuguezes do Século XVIII*, p.17

19 A.H.M.-DIV/1/7/1/30, Situation des Affaires du Portugal en 1762.

20 For Sarriá's proposal, see Mourinho, *Invasão de Trás-os-Montes e das Beiras*, p.394.

A carabineer from Lippe's guard. Sketch of a soldier from the guard of the Count of Lippe. This unit included two officers, five sergeants and 33 soldiers who came to Portugal together with the count (Drawing by Erich Dobrich, included in the book by Martin Lezius, *Das Ehrentleid des Soldaten*, Berlin: Verlag Ullstein, 1936).

was presumed to be aiming to take possession of the fortress of Almeida (as it later proved to have been the case), possession of which would have left them free to move west or south.[21] However, a number of hypothetical Bourbon options had to be considered.

One hypothesis was that, upon gaining access to the invasion line of the Mondego valley, the enemy might move on Coimbra. From there, access to Lisbon or Porto would be facilitated, given the better ground for advancement and the more abundant resources. Another hypothesis was that the enemy might search for an easier and more direct route to Lisbon to the south. This would also threaten the lengthy and vulnerable lines of communications, over which then both regular and irregular Portuguese forces had to act, causing serious damage. In this second hypothesis, the invading army would be in a better position to logistically give support to its own forces, while it would compel the Anglo-Portuguese army to split, as the latter would have to try to stop the invading forces at Almeida and to block another line of invasion further south. This solution would, furthermore, have the advantage of testing the real value of the Anglo-Portuguese Army, allowing the Bourbon powers to decide, once they had the measure of their oponents, which manoeuvre to follow later.

Yet another hypothesis was that the enemy might advance directly on the Anglo-Portuguese forces, with the purpose of destroying them. This option placed less importance on divining the enemy's final geographical objective which, after the failure of Trás-os-Montes, would appear to be Lisbon. As early as 20 May, in a letter on the shift of the theatre of operations from Trás-os-Montes to Beira, the Court in Aranjuez informed Sarriá about Carlos III's agreement with the proposals presented on the 16th and 17th of that month to attack the Anglo-Portuguese force: 'However, since that Province of Trás-os-Montes will be left unexplored now because Your Excellency, as well as the King, consider it preferable to seek and attack the body […] (and the King

21 A.H.M.-DIV/1/7/1/6, Projectos dos Espanhóis na Campanha de 1762. This document includes relevant considerations on the Spanish plans for invading Portugal.

Beira. Map of the province, published in the work by João Baptista de Castro, *Mappa de Portugal antigo e moderno, tomo I*, in 1762.

Abrantes was the place where the Count of Lippe set up his headquarters for the longest period of time during the war of 1762. Since it was a fundamental strategic centre, it was here that the Portuguese Army concentrated in April, up until the command by Marshal Conde-Barão was established. (English engraving based on a drawing made during the Peninsular War by Andrew Leith-Hay and published in *Narrative of the Peninsular War* in 1832)

approves) attacking and destroying these troops upon which the Portuguese rely for their project of opposition.'[22] In fact, what the Count of Lippe feared the most was that the enemy might only mask Almeida with a reduced force and might march with the bulk of the army against the Anglo-Portuguese.[23]

On the Portuguese side, concentrating the army in the central location around Abrantes, Tomar and Golegã, besides facilitating the meeting of the logistic units and means, implied an attitude of strategic expectation. It was up to the enemy to show their true intentions, so that they could be met appropriately. In fact, the Anglo-Portuguese Army, by being concentrated there, could shift its centre of gravity to the axis of invasion of Beira Alta, if the enemy came that way, or to the Alentejo region, which was a much easier terrain for the attacking army to advance through. In addition, by occupying this central position the Anglo-Portuguese Army could prevent the enemy's access to Abrantes and safeguard all crossings of the Tagus in that region. The latter could be expected to be essential if it needed to intervene south of the river or to balance forces between the two banks. This idea was so clear in Lippe's mind that, fourteen years after the campaign, in a letter that he sent to the Marquis of Pombal on 20 April 1776, he insisted that 'Abrantes is very important, especially for crossing the Tagus at a central point of the kingdom; one or more well-protected bridges must be established there'.[24] However, Lippe's plan was far bolder than this attitude of expectation might suggest. It involved an offensive action on the line of communications over Alcántara, Badajoz, Mérida and Caceres, so that, by taking the war to Spain, the Anglo-Portuguese might gain the initiative, boost the morale of their forces, harm the preparations for a possible operation further south, and oblige the enemy to deploy forces to deal with this action. As Lippe mentioned in his *Memoir*, through these objectives, 'not only did the operations against Almeida slacken, but the project of the invasion of Alentejo was possibly frustrated in this campaign'.[25]

The Marshal-General's plan was reminiscent of the debate that had taken place in Abrantes between Nuno Álvares Pereira and the members of the Council of João I, before the battle of Aljubarrota in 1385, which chronicler Fernão Lopes well described. While Pereira advocating barring the progression of the Castilian troops, thus preventing them from reaching Lisbon, since 'once Lisbon was lost, the whole kingdom was lost', the majority of the Council proposed that an offensive action be taken over Andalusia. As we know, Pereira's idea eventually prevailed, and the Castilian forces were defeated in Aljubarrota.

These plans contain a degree of similarity. Firstly, Abrantes was the central point in both. Furthermore, Lippe's plan contained elements from

22 'Carta da Corte para o Marquês de Sarriá, de 20 de Maio de 1762', in Mourinho, *Invasão de Trás-os-Montes e das Beiras*, pp.410-411.

23 Anon. 'Carta do Conde de Lippe para o Conde de Oeiras, de 19 de Setembro', p.243.

24 Pereira Sales, *O Conde de Lippe*, p. 189n, refers to the fact that this letter was published in *O Investigador Portuguêz em Inglaterra*, Vol. II, London: 1811-1812, pp.548-551.

25 Schaumbourg-Lippe, 'Memória sobre a Campanha de 1762', pp.185-186.

Alentejo. Map of the province, published in the work by João Baptista de Castro, *Mappa de Portugal antigo e moderno, tomo I*, in 1762.

both opposing theses. On the one hand, it included offensive action in Spain, on the basis of the idea, which the Count referred to in his *Memoir*:

> [T]he intention of the enemy was to invade the Alentejo, after the capture of Almeida, but it had hitherto postponed this plan, because of the tremendous drought in that province, which was short of water in the summer months. The Spanish had 3 or 4,000 men who were stationed in many towns and villages between the Tagus and the Guadiana, mainly in locations that were close to Alcantara and the River Sabor;[26] warehouses started to be set up there; many ammunition depots and victual storehouses had already been established in various places of Spanish Extremadura; and convoys of all kinds continuously covered the large road between Badajoz and the Army, which besieged Almeida.[27]

On the other hand, Lippe's plan did not neglect to focus on monitoring and defending the gorges along the line of invasion of Beira Alta, thus barring, like Pereira in 1385, the access to Lisbon.

In order to implement this plan on the ground, the Count of Lippe placed a force under the command of Lieutenant General Townshend in the region of Viseu. By mid-August, this force had at its disposal the Infantry Regiment of Moura, eight other Portuguese infantry battalions, one British infantry battalion, and the Regiment of Royal Volunteers (recently set up at the expense of personnel from the existing infantry and cavalry regiments), which occupied and re-established the fortifications of Celorico da Beira, one detachment of dragoons led by Burgoyne, and 10 cannon. This body was reinforced, later, with a force under the command of Brigadier Lennox: the Regiment of Dragoons of Chaves, four battalions, and several units from the province of Minho.

A force was set up in the Guarda region with the mission of covering the region of Beira Baixa and bringing 'wheat, forage and cattle' to the rear, for the purpose of hampering the logistics of the enemy's army. This force, under the command of Major General the Count of Santiago, consisted of one infantry regiment, one cavalry regiment, two infantry battalions and six cannons. As for the offensive action in Spain, the Count of Lippe intended to carry it out with the bulk of the Anglo-Portuguese Army, which consisted of 17 infantry battalions and four cavalry regiments, with artillery.[28]

As often is the case, what happened differed from what had been planned by the two armies. On 30 July, the Franco-Spanish Army, under the command of the Marquis of Sarriá, entered Portuguese territory and approached Almeida, the fortress on the axis of invasion of Beira Alta with the best conditions for defence, whose conquest was necessary in order to

26 This is one of several incorrect geographical references in the Memoir. While they are understandable on the part of the Count of Lippe, they are less excusable on the part of Manuel de Arriaga, his secretary. The river he wished to mention must have been the Sever or the Salor, tributaries of the right bank of the Tagus, and not the Sabor, a tributary of the right bank of the Douro.

27 Schaumbourg-Lippe, 'Memória sobre a Campanha de 1762', p.185.

28 Information about the plan can be viewed in Pereira Sales, *O Conde de Lippe*, pp.16-19.

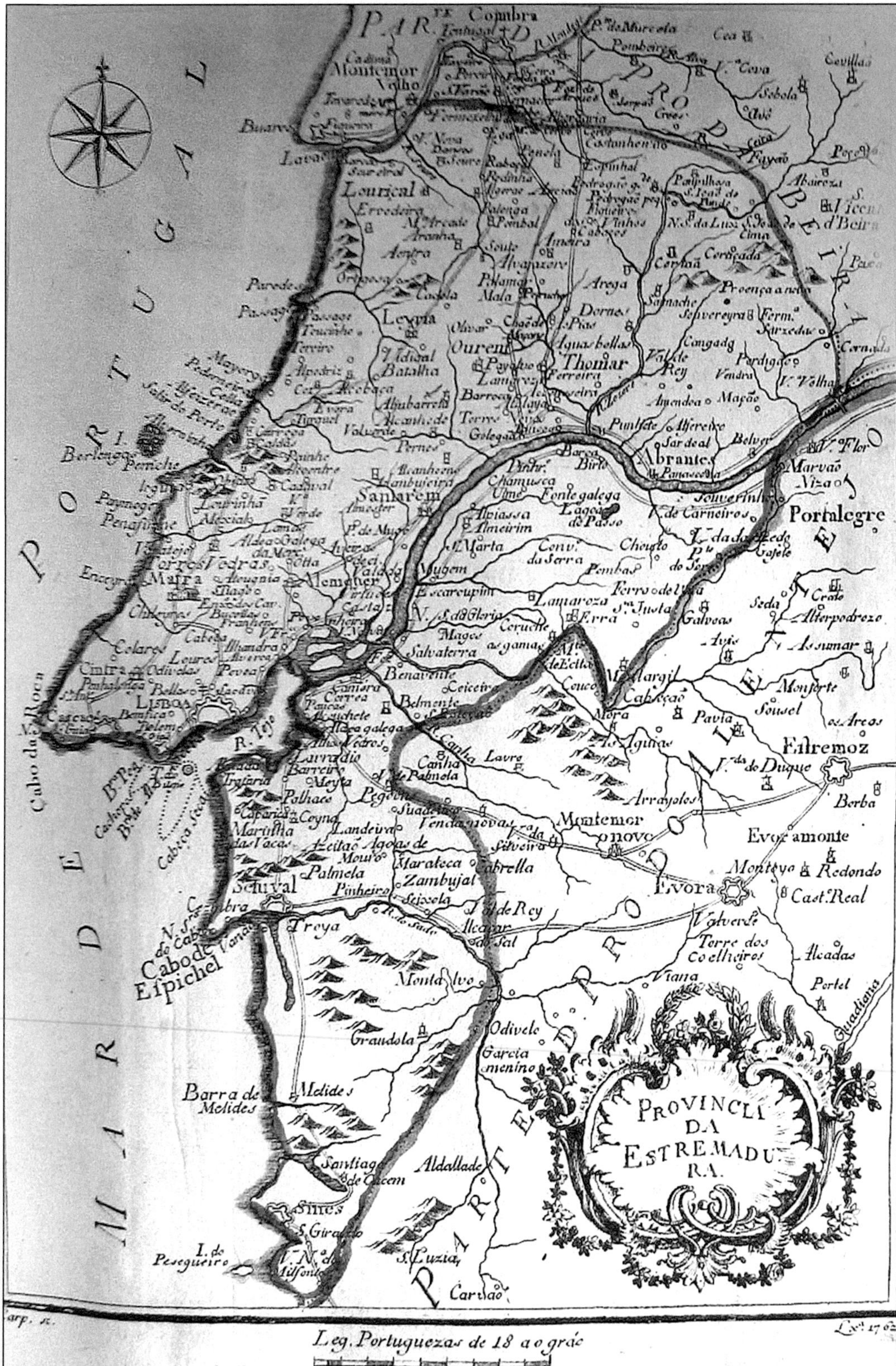


Estremadura. Map of the province, published in the work by João Baptista de Castro, *Mappa de Portugal antigo e moderno*, *tomo I*, in 1762.

Luís de Albuquerque de Melo Cáceres (c. 1739-1797) participated in the War of 1762 as an officer of the cavalry regiment of Almeida. Later, in April 1764, he was appointed to the staff of General Francis McClean (1717-1781). In 1771, at the age of 31, he was appointed Governor and Captain-General of the Captainship of Mato Grosso e Cuiabá in Brazil and carried out this function until 1789. The text of the legend in the lower right part of the painting reads: 'Luís de Albuquerque de Melo Pereira e Cáceres, Nobleman from the House of His Most Faithful Majesty and Infantry Captain serving as adjutant to General Francis McLean'. (Unsigned and undated painting, José Joaquim Diabazal Collection – House of Ínsua)

use this axis. By 4 August, the invading forces were close to Almeida and the day after they began to besiege it.

> Almeida is a quasi-regular hexagon, its enclosure, scarp and counterscarp are covered with thick stonework; its moats are dry but deep; its bulwarks are full and spacious; there are half-moons facing all the fronts, and a road protected from fire encircles the fort; there are no places in its vicinity that dominate it, from which the fort cannot easily disentangle itself. Inside the settlement there is a castle, which is surrounded by deep ditches and cannot be beaten until after the settlement has been taken; one of the bulwarks is bombproof and can accommodate 1,000 men within.[29]

The Governor of the fort was Major General Alexandre Palhares Coelho de Brito, who, at the time, was 81 years old, 'an age that was not very appropriate for the good performance of such an arduous task'.[30] Its garrison consisted of two battalions of the Regiment of Almeida, one cavalry regiment with 150 horses, four tercios made up of auxiliary personnel, and one artillery corps, to a total of around 3,000 men.[31] It had enough artillery, ammunition, and supplies to withstand for some time. Sooner or later, if no reinforcements arrived or if the siege units were diverted for other action, the fortress would have to surrender, given the force of the invading army (which had about 40,000 men and was well supported by artillery and mortars).

The Count of Lippe's plan for an offensive against Spanish Extremadura, which had as one further purpose that of forcing the enemy to divert its forces away from Almeida, thus alleviating the siege, was based on the premise that the fortress should resist for some time. For this reason, the Marshal-General ordered the governor of the fort not to surrender for as long as the enemy did not open a breach in the walls through which 'a line of 30 men' could pass.

On 7 August, Castelo Rodrigo, which had a garrison of only 40 men, surrendered. On 11 August, with the approach of two companies and 30 horses, the Governor of Alfaiates, Simão Monteiro, who thought that 'the power of the enemy was much greater, delivered the fort without engaging in the slightest effort of defence',[32] and left the enemy six guns and some ammunition,[33] a fact which the Count of Lippe commented with bitterness in a letter he sent to the Count of Oeiras.[34] Two days later, there was an attempt by common people to recover Alfaiates, but firing from the occupants of the

29 Schaumbourg-Lippe, 'Memória sobre a Campanha de 1762', p.184.

30 Pereira Sales, *O Conde de Lippe*, p.38.

31 Pereira Sales, *O Conde de Lippe*, p.35 referred to around 2,000 men, but mentioned only one tercio made up of auxiliary personnel. In Conde de Schaumbourg-Lippe, 'Memória sobre a Campanha de 1762', p.184, reference is made to around 3,000 men; A.H.M.-DIV/1/7/2/24: Correspondência do Sargento-Mor Alexandre Palhares, reference is made to four tercios made up of auxiliary personnel but not to the total number of men; and *Historia de España*, p.82 states that the fort had a garrison of 4,000 men, undoubtedly to enhance the importance of the conquest that had been made.

32 A.H.M.-DIV/1/7/2/24, Carta de D. Marques de Noronha, Conde dos Arcos, Governador de Armas da Beira, a D. Luís da Cunha, Secretário de Estado dos Negócios da Guerra.

33 A.H.M.-DIV/1/7/1/30, Situation des Affaires du Portugal en 1762.

34 Anon. 'Carta do Conde de Lippe para o Conde de Oeiras, de 19 de Setembro', p.252.

fort forced them to withdraw with some injured. This action is described in a letter from the Marshal-General to the Count of Oeiras. Finding that the surrender of the fort by his garrison, when he had 'cannon and ammunition', had been shameful, the Marshal-General viewed the action of the people, who 'with all intrepidity had thrown themselves in with their naked chests',[35] as their condemnation of the unworthy surrender that the Governor had accepted.

In mid-August, while the command of the Anglo-Portuguese Army knew about the Spanish attempt to take Almeida, it had no idea of what the direction of the invading army's effort would be. Because of this, the Count of Lippe insisted to the Count of Oeiras that logistic facilities might be organised so as to guarantee support for the forces in Coimbra and Viseu (in case the war effort were to be carried out in Beira Alta) but also in Santarém, Punhete (now Constância), Tomar and Abrantes (in case the war effort was carried out in Beira Baixa or Alentejo).[36]

In the first days of August, the bulk of the Anglo-Portuguese Army was concentrated in the region of the Zêzere and of Abrantes, to carry out the planned offensive action on Spanish territory. On 24 August, the march-order was issued.[37] The force was made up of three regiments of cavalry and eight infantry regiments. Having crossed the Tagus, it proceeded towards Gavião, which it reached on the 26th. Two days later, it arrived in Nisa, where headquarters were established. Due to logistical shortcomings, this journey was painful for the troops, which led the Count of Lippe to express his satisfaction with the way in which the personnel had endured hardship.

Brigadier John Burgoyne (1722-1792). Commander of the 16th Light Dragons, established in 1759 and the first regiment of light cavalry of the British Army. His regiment was the only cavalry unit of the British expeditionary force that was sent to Portugal in 1762. Burgoyne later famously surrendered in Saratoga, on 17 October 1777, during the War of American Independence.

The words which the Count used to commend the units were among the Marshal-General's first public demonstrations he made about the behaviour of the personnel and the units under his command. He praised all that was remarkable and showed a spirit of good service and condemned mistakes and lack of military spirit. In fact, this was one of the ways in which he exercised his command. He encouraged military virtues and praised discipline, both of which he defined as essential characteristics for an efficient army. Military performance by Burgoyne and his dragoons was also noteworthy. After a long march, they entered Valencia de Alcántara by surprise, and there they made around 200 prisoners, captured three flags of the Seville Regiment, and destroyed provisions of the enemy's army. Following this action, Burgoyne, now reinforced with a British infantry regiment and

35 Anon. 'Carta do Conde de Lippe para o Conde de Oeiras, de 19 de Setembro', p.250.
36 Anon. 'Carta do Conde de Lippe para o Conde de Oeiras, de 19 de Setembro', p.254.
37 A.H.M.-DIV/1/7/1/35: Ordens dadas pelo Conde de Schaumbourg Lippe que se executaram na Campanha de 1762.

a Portuguese cavalry regiment, was given the task of covering the border between Vila Velha de Ródão and Portalegre.

On 23 August, the Count of Lippe announced to Lisbon that the enemy had opened a trench in the night of the15th-16th, in front of the bastions of Santo António and São Pedro, at around 300 *toises*[38] away from the road protected from fire of the fortress of Almeida.[39] However, on his side, he had installed, on the 12th, one battery with 14 mortars; on the 17th, one battery with 16 cannon and another with 14 (24-pound) cannon; and, on the 23rd, one battery with 10 guns and two batteries with mortars.

On the 31st, the command of the army received the news that the fort of Almeida had surrendered on the 25th. The Governor of Almeida said that he had been 'obliged to capitulate because he was faced with an open breach and the lack of a garrison that might have been capable to fight against any assault initiated by the enemies', but the Count of Arcos, in a letter to the Secretary of State for War Affairs, stated that 'there was no evidence of a lack of supplies, or even of powder and bullets'.[40]

The fall of Almeida forced the cancellation of the offensive action, so as to permit a return of the disposable forces to their initial position, in the region of Abrantes, and to reinforce the troops in the valley of the Mondego, in order to increase the capacity of defence along that line of invasion. It was these successive occupations of the region of Abrantes that generated the popular saying '*Tudo velho como dantes, Quartel-General em Abrantes*' meaning 'All the same as before, headquarters at Abrantes'.

What had happened in Almeida had been a premature surrender, in view of the fact that not all the means and capacities that existed and might allow to resist for more time had been used. Alexandre de Palhares had been appointed Governor of the fortress of Almeida, the most important border fort (together with Elvas), without regard to his advanced age. Defence of the fort did not unfold as expected. The Count of Lippe had ordered him, as already mentioned, not to surrender before there was a large breach on the wall. Furthermore, he had recommended the removal of the civilian population in order to save food. McClean, a competent officer, who was later promoted to the post of major general, had been sent as an advisor to the governor. McClean and the regiment's commander, Fernando Costa Atayde (an officer whom the Count referred to as having acted with distinction,[41]) had intended to prolong the effort of defence. However, in the end what happened was that the governor did not remove the civilian population from the fort; could not avoid desertion by the auxiliaries; did not refrain from allowing the nuns to shelter in the bunker, leaving the military exposed to the enemy's bombings; and did not listen to the advice of those who were more determined than he was to prolong the effort of defence. After a little more than two weeks of siege and an exchange of artillery shots, and 'in spite of the

38 1 toise = 1.949 m.

39 Anon. 'Carta do Conde de Lippe para o Conde de Oeiras, de 19 de Setembro', p.259.

40 Carta do Conde dos Arcos para D. Luís da Cunha, de 4 de Setembro de 1762, in A.H.M.-DIV/1/7/2/24, Correspondência do Sargento-Mor Alexandre Palhares.

41 Anon. 'Carta do Conde de Lippe para o Conde de Oeiras, de 19 de Setembro', p.263.

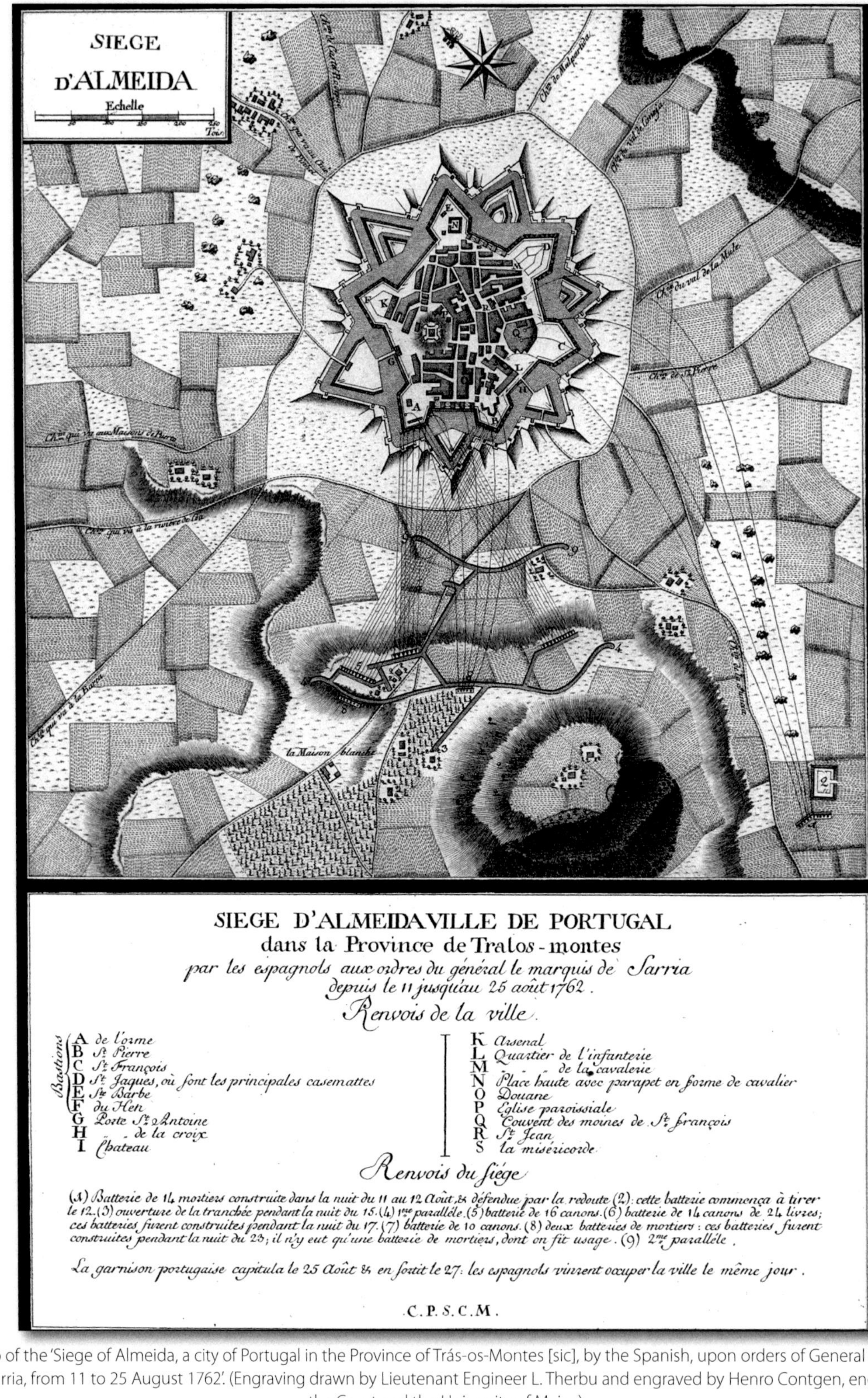


Map of the 'Siege of Almeida, a city of Portugal in the Province of Trás-os-Montes [sic], by the Spanish, upon orders of General Marquis of Sarria, from 11 to 25 August 1762'. (Engraving drawn by Lieutenant Engineer L. Therbu and engraved by Henro Contgen, engraver at the Court and the University of Mainz)

The capture of Almeida. The fortress of Almeida surrendered on 25 August 1762. As a consequence of this feat, the Spanish commander, the Marquis of Sarria, was awarded the Order of the Golden Fleece. (Drawing attributed to Cavaleiro Faria in *Notícias dos Sucessos da Guerra de Hespanha…* (News on the developments in the Spanish War…), belonging to the Library of the Military Academy, Lisbon, doc. 2058).

fact that the enemy was only at the first parallel and the damage caused by his artillery was limited, [the Governor] summoned the council of officers, the majority of whom voted for capitulation, which in fact occurred on 25 August'.[42]

One of Almeida's garrison officers, Lieutenant Marques Cardoso, highlighted, in a book he later wrote, the high level of desertion on the part of the auxiliaries and their relevance as source of information for the enemy.[43] He also stated (in an account of dubious accuracy, presumably written down by a supporter of the invading army) that:

> [A]fter a considerable loss of people by desertions and deaths in various ways, as soon as they began digging the trench, and those besieged tried preventing this work with some fire, the Duke of Baños, who was at the service of the Generalissimo, the Marquis of Sarreá, informed him in the following way: Excellency, Lord, the fire is so violent that the fort has turned us into the besieged and, if this does or we do not stop them, we will need to return to Spain, or we will all remain here.[44]

Contrary to what had happened with the Governor of Almeida, this possible advice was not heeded by the Marquis, who continued the siege until the fort's surrender.

## From Almeida to the Tagus Crossing Attempt

The conquest of Almeida by the forces of the Franco-Spanish Army led the Count of Lippe to reconsider the planned offensive action on Spanish Extremadura and to work on having the bulk of the army return to the region of the Zêzere and Abrantes. On 2 September, he initiated a march, together with four British regiments, 'to free the Royal Highway of Coimbra, and help Lieutenant General Townshend'.[45] He also ordered a force of around 2,500 men and six cannons, under the command of Lieutenant General Dom Luis de Portugal, to march over the Mondego valley. According to Ernesto Pereira Sales, this force should have had more 6,000 men, on the basis of its required operational numbers. This means that, once again, one finds that the actual numbers were far fewer than they should have been, which necessarily affected the operational capacity of the forces.[46]

The second force departed on 4 September and, after a troubled march, during which logistics and command capacity failed, it arrived on 8 September in Miranda do Corvo. Some shortcomings were identified. These led the Count of Lippe to write a highly critical comment on the service

42 Pereira Sales, *O Conde de Lippe*, pp.36-37.
43 José Marques Cardoso, *Elementos da Arte da Guerra* (Lisboa: Offic. Patr. De Francisco Luiz Ameno, 1785), pp.100-101.
44 Cardoso, *Elementos da Arte da Guerra*, p.119.
45 Anon. 'Carta do Conde de Lippe para o Conde de Oeiras, de 19 de Setembro', p.262.
46 Pereira Sales, *O Conde de Lippe*, p.20.

order of 8 September.[47] On 11 September, the force was assigned the task of occupying the estuary of the Arouce. On the next day, it dispatched a battalion to the Mucela bridge on the Alva river, which was a mandatory passage for any forces on the left bank of the Mondego wishing to advance through the axis from Celorico da Beira to Coimbra via Oliveira do Hospital. This battalion relieved the British unit that had been at this position before. By doing this, the Marshal-General reinforced the operation that Townshend was carrying out for the purpose of defending the invasion line of Beira Alta.

The Marquis of Sarriá, sensing that the King of Spain was unhappy with the way in which he had been running the military operations, asked for his resignation shortly after Almeida was taken, invoking lack of health and advanced age. His resignation was accepted, he received the Order of the Golden Fleece, and on 4 September he was replaced by the Count of Aranda in the command of the Franco-Spanish Army.

After Almeida's surrender, the Franco-Spanish Army resumed its progression over Celorico da Beira, but it soon veered to the south. One division marched towards Alcântara and the remainder of that portion of the army that had entered Portuguese territory advanced towards Sabugal and Penamacor. On 16 September, the Count of Aranda, by then already in Penamacor, informed the Court that he was marching south for the purpose of taking possession of Castelo Branco, on a manoeuvre that received the King's approval.[48] The command of the invading army was possibly considering imitating a manoeuvre by Philip V, which had occurred during the War of the Spanish Succession of Spain around 60 years before, and which Ferreira Martins described as follows:

> Filipe V rushed in from Madrid to Plasencia and from there to Alcántara, with an army that was commanded by the Marshal of France, the Duke of Berwick. The army invaded the Portuguese border of Beira, seized Castelo Branco, and moved on with the purpose of advancing on Abrantes, on what was the first attempt of invasion through the right bank of the Tagus onto Lisbon. Nevertheless, it ran up against the Talhadas mountain, between Vila-Velha and the Zêzere, which forced it to stop and to wait until a body of troops, which had entered the territory through the Alentejo border, might reach it by advancing along the left bank of the Tagus.
>
> Berwick recognised that it was impossible to proceed with the ongoing march on the right bank. He therefore crossed the Tagus in Vila-Velha and took Marvão and Portalegre. While the Count of S. Vicente, the military governor for Alentejo, sought to free these forts, the Marquis of Minas (António Luís de Sousa, Second Marquis of Minas), governor of Beira, marched from Almeida and beat the enemy troops that were occupying Beira Baixa in Monsanto.[49]

47 Pereira Sales, *O Conde de Lippe*, p.30.

48 'Carta do Rei para o Conde de Aranda, de 20 de Setembro de 1762', in Mourinho, *Invasão de Trás-os-Montes e das Beiras*, p.398.

49 Ferreira Martins, *História do Exército Português*, p.165.

On 14 September, due to the southward diversion of the invading army, the Count of Lippe ordered the withdrawal to Abrantes of the units that had been sent to reinforce the contingent under Lieutenant General Townshend and to occupy Foz de Arouce and the Mucela bridge. Then, in the following days, he rearranged the dispositions of the Anglo-Portuguese army.

Lieutenant General Townshend positioned the force under his command in the region of Celorico da Beira, thus covering the valley of the Mondego. The Count of Santiago covered Beira Baixa and, given his mission to keep it 'for as long as possible', he establishes his command at Alcains. Burgoyne followed his mission of covering the area between the Tagus and Portalegre and installed his command in Tolosa, to the south of Nisa. Most of the British units, under the command of Lord Loudoun, were in reserve in the Sardoal region. The headquarters and the remaining forces of the general reserve were in the region of Abrantes.

On 17 September, near the border, Salvaterra surrendered as soon as it was instructed to by the enemy, despite the order that the Governor had received to resist, unless resistance became impossible. Segura, which possessed no means of defence, also surrendered.[50] These two forts guaranteed to the enemy's army safe passage through the river Erges, allowing for easy access from Alcántara to Castelo Branco, the region where a large part of the invading army's units soon were to gather.

As a consequence of the successes of the Franco-Spanish Army, the Count of Lippe pondered that the enemy might try to cross the Tagus near Vila Velha de Ródão, so as to conduct operations in the Alentejo and later advance towards Lisbon, or, alternatively, might progress along the right bank of the Tagus, onto Tomar and Abrantes, and continue towards Lisbon. The latter was the manoeuvre made by General Junot around 50 years later, during the first French invasion, although he did not encounter any opposition. Of these two possibilities, the one that the Count of Lippe feared the most was that of the territory's invasion via Alentejo:

> First, because this Province is on its own less strong than the northern parts of the country. Second, because the enemy's manoeuvres in this part of the country will conduct it directly to the heart of the Kingdom, this is, the Estuary of the Tagus. Thirdly, because the commoners, who are so useful in the mountains, will not be able, in spite of their good will, to render such solid services in this Province.[51]

Under these circumstances, and taking into consideration both possibilities, the Count of Lippe manoeuvred the Anglo-Portuguese Army in order to oppose them.

Using the forces under the Count of Santiago were assigned to bar the enemy's access to the region of Abrantes by defending the passageways of the River Ocreza and of the mountain ranges of Talhadas, Alvelos and Moradal. In a letter to the Count of Oeiras, of 19 Setember, Lippe praised the Count of Santiago, stating that, in spite of the lack of high rank personnel,

---

50 Pereira Sales, *O Conde de Lippe*, p.21.

51 Anon. 'Carta do Conde de Lippe para o Conde de Oeiras, de 19 de Setembro', p.255.

Portugal still possessed some military leaders of superior competence and devotion. Making Santiago's task easier, since there were only two lines by which the enemy might penetrate further into Portugal. One of them started in Sarzedas, Alvito and Sobreira Formosa and followed a path that overall coincides with what is now the road from Castelo Branco to Proença-a-Nova and Abrantes. The other, located more to the north, began in Sarnadas de S. Simão and continued in the direction of Sertã via Oleiros. The Count of Lippe instructed Lieutenant General Townshend, who had advanced towards the River Côa and was in the Pinhel region, to march south, while leaving Lord Lennox behind, with four Portuguese infantry regiments, the Dragoon of Chaves, the remnant of the Almeida Cavalry, and the Royal Volunteer Regiment, so as to keep a watch over Almeida. In order to prevent the enemy army from crossing the Tagus, he ordered Brigadier Burgoyne to continue to monitor the River Sever, so as to avoid any surprise should the enemy attempt any manoeuvre in that region, and to bar the passage of enemy forces south of the Tagus. For the purpose of defence, he also determined the occupation and fortification of a strong point in the region of the castle of Vila Velha de Ródão. The command and the bulk of the army advanced towards the region of Mação, in order to be able either to support to the defence effort or cover the withdrawal of the installed forces should the enemy attack the passageways in the mountains.

Through this commitment which the army placed on the defence of Beira Baixa, the Marshal-General aimed to make the enemy believe that the Anglo-Portuguese Army was more fearful of another movement against Abrantes than of the crossing of the Franco-Spanish Army to the south of the Tagus. The Count of Lippe said in his *Memoir* that:

> [A]fter these measures had been taken to prevent the crossing of the Tagus at Vila Velha [...], one would presume [...] that, ashamed of making a backward march with such superior forces, the flattering idea of moving straight to the capital would induce it to cross those mountains and march on Abrantes and on the crossings of the Zêzere. This last move [...] was for us the least dangerous and could cause the annihilation of the enemy's army.[52]

This is to say that the Count of Lippe wished that the enemy would not have its army return to Alcántara (where the bridge was one of the main and most important works made by the Romans in the Iberian Peninsula and bears an inscription that reveals that Lusitania started there), to then cross to the south of the Tagus, for this would make the country's defence almost impossible, since the invading army was more numerous and had a large cavalry contingent and the terrain in Alentejo did not favour the defence.

The Count of Aranda, who kept much of his army in the region of Castelo Branco, sent a force of around 6,000 men to the Tagus in the proximity of Vila Velha de Ródão. While this force tried to find passageways across the river, it fortified some positions, from which it fired on the units of Brigadier

52 Schaumbourg-Lippe, 'Memória sobre a Campanha de 1762', p.432.

Burgoyne in the attempt to erode the defences on the southern bank of the Tagus.[53] Another force of around 4,000 men left Castelo Branco by the royal road and took position in the region of Sarzedas, opposite the positions of Alvito which were occupied by units of the Count of Santiago. One further force, of 2-3,000 men, moved more northwards, along the road from Pampilhosa to the region of São Simão, on the road to Oleiros, which was also garrisoned with a battalion.[54]

The military dispositions of the Franco-Spanish Army, close to the hills, can be interpreted as a covering force that guaranteed the security of the right flank of the army during the crossing of the Tagus. In fact, however, it can also be considered as an early formulation of a disposition for an offensive operation towards the west, in the direction of Abrantes. From the correspondence that was exchanged between Aranda and the Spanish Court between 23 and 29 September, this was in fact what was planned.[55]

## Effort in Beira Baiza

Franco-Spanish Army units by the Tagus headed an attack on the advanced positions that were defending the castle of Vila Velha de Ródão. Consequently, Brigadier Burgoyne, who occupied positions on the left bank, had some British infantry companies cross over to the other bank for the purpose of reinforcing the defence of the village castle. However, these advanced positions succumbed after five hours of combat and, before the reinforcement reached its destination, on October 2, the commander of Vila Velha, Lieutenant-Colonel Azevedo Coutinho, with his garrison of around 350 men, surrendered. The Count of Lippe considered in his *Memoir* that, after the fall of the outposts, it was not possible to maintain the position of the castle. All the same, he regretted that the commander had not joined Burgoyne's command, rather than allowing his men to become captives.[56]

Due to the continued presence of the forces of Burgoyne, which were positioned on the left bank of the Tagus, the enemy force was not able to take control of a crossing point even though it held Vila Velha de Ródão. On October 3, the force once again moved on and, on passing through Porto Cabrão,[57] threatened the cohesion of the Anglo-Portuguese army's dispositions. However, the units that were in Sarzedas, under the command of the Count of Torre, advanced on Alvito, seeking to involve the forces of

53 Mourinho, *Invasão de Trás-os-Montes e das Beiras*, p 399.

54 The numbers, mentioned here, of the columns of the Franco-Spanish Army, which imposed a defensive position on the Anglo-Portuguese Army, between Sarnadas de São Simão and Vila Velha do Ródão, are those indicated in Schaumbourg-Lippe, 'Memória sobre a Campanha de 1762', p.537. It has not proved possible to confirm these figures in other sources.

55 'Cartas de Aranda ao Rei e de Carlos III a Aranda, do arquivo de Simancas', in Mourinho, *Invasão de Trás-os-Montes e das Beiras*, p.399.

56 Conde de Schaumbourg-Lippe, 'Memória sobre a Campanha de 1762', p. 538.

57 This was the name of the place then, as included in contemporary maps and in the Memoir of the Count of Lippe and reproduced in Pereira Sales's book. Nowadays the area is named Ribeira do Cobrão and Foz do Cobrão.

The Combat at Alvito. Battle between the Portuguese forces of the Count of Santiago and the Spanish forces that had set up a camp at Sarzedas. It occurred on 3 October 1762 while the Portuguese forces were withdrawing form Alvito and were heading towards Sobreira Formosa. (Drawing attributed to Cavaleiro Faria in *Notícias dos Sucessos da Guerra de Hespanha…* (News on the developments in the Spanish War…), belonging to the Library of the Military Academy, Lisbon, doc. 2058, p. 245)

the Count of Santiago. To the north, in Sarnadas de São Simão, a detachment that had arrived there, after being reinforced, undertook an offensive action towards Oleiros. These attitudes by the forces of the Franco-Spanish Army, following their frustrated attempts to cross the Tagus, showed their determination to move westwards.

In this context, the Marshal-General reinforced the Count of Santiago's body with two battalions, sent four British infantry regiments to the region of Sobreira Formosa, and occupied the Talhadas heights. These were a mountainous barrier that was difficult to cross and easy to defend and which, from northwest to southeast, included a section from the Serra do Moradal to the Tagus, close to Vila Velha de Ródão, and then extended to the south of this river up until the area of Nisa. This is why the Marshal-General said: 'I have sent the British troops of Lord Loudon up until close to where the Conde of Santiago is stationed […] The withdrawal was carried out successfully'.[58] Then, together with elements from the four British regiments that were at the Talhadas reinforced with Portuiguse detachments and two cannon, he set up a rear-guard. At the same time that the Anglo-Portuguese army was retreating, the enemy was resuming its advance at a slow pace, due to the difficulties of the terrain and to the resistance made by the opposing army.

On the side of the Anglo-Portuguese forces, two facts occurred that are worth mentioning. One of them took place after the capture of Vila Velha.

58 A.H.M., DIV-1/7/2/9, Notas sobre as Operações Militares…

The enemy force, under the command of the Count of Huesca, resumed its progression, as mentioned before, but left around 200 men, 100 horses and mules, and six cannon behind, near the village. Brigadier Burgoyne, who had been given the mission of hampering enemy action, ordered a coup de main against the enemy camp near the village, which was carried out by around 300 grenadiers, most of them Portuguese, under the command of Colonel Lee.[59] This operation caused a high number of casualties and prisoners, as well as the seizure of the mules and the destruction of the cannons, and the surprise factor was such that the enemy's dispositive in the village was only reinforced on the following day.

The other fact that needs to be mentioned was the conduction of two marches which Lieutenant General Townshend carried out with the units under his command. The fact was that the direction taken by the Franco-Spanish Army had shifted considerably after the capture of Almeida. Townshend was therefore instructed to march along 250 kilometres of arduous paths, from the region of Pinhel to Codes, north of Mação, which was a waiting and a blocking position on the road from Sardoal to Proença-a-Nova. Shortly after the force had arrived there, which signalled to the enemy a wish to advance on Abrantes, the Count of Lippe once again ordered Townshend and his units to leave, since he already held a strong position in the area between the Zêzere, the region of Codes and the Tagus (which was defensible with little personnel). This time they were to march on the right bank of the Zêzere up until Pampilhosa da Serra, and then move eastward so as to join the forces of Lord Lennox, who had been sent south via Guarda and Belmonte for the purpose of cutting the enemy's line of communications with Almeida and Ciudad Rodrigo and creating a threat to the other line that had now been created via Alcántara and Castelo Branco. This new march, which was carried out through a path of around 200 kilometres of difficult terrain, was the object of praise by the Count of Lippe, who highlighted 'the admirable perseverance of the Portuguese soldier, who endured the greatest hardships and who, nevertheless, happily wandered through those paths with sharp rocks, leaving traces everywhere of his bleeding feet!'[60]

On 8 October, the Count of Lippe informed the Count of Oeiras that it was now clear that the invading army, unable to cross the Tagus, intended to reach Abrantes with its full force. However, to be able to do so it would need to progress through a terrain that facilitated defence and thus made it very difficult for the Bourbon forces to attain their objective.

The bulk of the invading army had advanced from the region of Castelo Branco to the Sarzedas heights, where it established a new headquarters. The force that was there had advanced beyond Sobreira Formosa, had made reconnaissance raids to Cardigas, and had sought to improve the itineraries with the intention of facilitating tactical displacements and securing logistical support. To the north from there, the Count of Torre and the units under his command advanced from Sarnadas de São Simão to Oleiros. However, these

59 Ernesto Pereira Sales noted that the grenadiers were Portuguese. In contrast, the Count of Lippe observed in his memoir that they were British. See Pereira Sales, *O Conde de Lippe*, p.25n.

60 Schaumbourg-Lippe, 'Memória sobre a Campanha de 1762', p.542.

advances by the enemy, which the Count of Lippe did his best to hamper with the units under his command, showed the vulnerabilities of the mode of action that the Franco-Spanish army had chosen to take. First of all, one must mention the difficult terrain and the use made by the Anglo-Portuguese army of its excellent defensive positions. In addition to that, the invading army needed to have all its logistical support sent from Spain, because the Count of Santiago, following the instructions he had received from the Marshal-General, had withdrawn or destroyed any means of subsistence which the enemy might use in its area of intervention. Moreover, the reprisals that the invading army, particularly the French forces,[61] had wrought on the local people, causing deaths and igniting fires, led these to take revenge on any isolated elements they encountered. Thus, 'on this occasion, terrible cruelties were practiced by one side and the other'.[62]

Because some enemy detachments were approaching Codes, which was a key terrain in the line of defence that protected Abrantes, the Anglo-Portuguese army had to to occupy all the positions that could bar the enemy's progression. The land between the Tagus and the Zêzere provided an excellent defensive position

> [B]ecause, although its left side relies on the Codos, which joins the Zêzere at a short distance from S. Domingos, the banks of this stream, from its origin to its confluence with the Zêzere, are so steep, that it was very easy to prevent any attempt of passage: thus, all the avenues of approach to the fort of Abrantes were occupied. This position always dominates the entire territory lying ahead, and the mountains that make part of it are in many places, to the side of the enemy, like curtains cut straight down in living rock [whilst] to our side these same mountains have smooth slopes that allowed and very much facilitated the manoeuvres of the troops and of the artillery, covering them from the enemy's sight, to the extent that they reinforced, in some cases, the most strongly threatened points.[63]

In this context, on October 15 the enemy's most advanced forces began to retreat to Sarzedas and Vila Velha de Ródão while the bulk of its army withdrew to Castelo Branco. In fact, this happened for all the reasons mentioned above, which hindered the enemy's advance, but also because of the level of exhaustion which its units were experiencing, due to diseases, desertions and logistical difficulties, which were further aggravated by their dependence only on the umbilical cord from Segura to Castelo Branco, which was also liable to be cut off by Lieutenant General Townshend.

---

61 The Count of Aranda complained, in letters he sent to the Court in November, about the way in which the French forces were acting and oppressing the population. Mourinho, *Invasão de Trás-os-Montes e das Beiras*, p.399.

62 Schaumbourg-Lippe, 'Memória sobre a Campanha de 1762', p.541.

63 Schaumbourg-Lippe, 'Memória sobre a Campanha de 1762', p.543.

## From Retreat to Peace

The Franco-Spanish Army was unable to cross to the south of the Tagus in Portuguese territory and gave up progressing along the right bank of this river towards Abrantes. As a result of this, its forces retreated and gradually gathered and reorganised in the region of Castelo Branco. While some units returned to Spain, the enemy did not withdraw completely from Beira Baixa, seeming to wish to continue to occupy a significant part of this province.

At the end of October, cavalry units withdrew by the road of Ladoeiro, Zebreira and Segura, and continued until Alcántara, where they crossed over to the left bank of the Tagus. These forces were followed by infantry and artillery units. There was also a body of 12 battalions that marched to Malpica do Tejo and then, having crossed the river on barges, proceeded to Herrera de Alcántara, where it joined other troops coming from the south. Nevertheless, despite the withdrawal of these units, a part of the Franco-Spanish Army remained in place at cantonments and barracks throughout the region of Castelo Branco.

In order to keep in contact with the enemy, persecute him and cause him damage, the Count of Lippe sent a force of four battalions and two cavalry regiments, under the command of Major General Fraser. This mission was not successful because abundant rains made the crossing of the rivers difficult. Brigadier Burgoyne reoccupied Vila Velha de Ródão. Lieutenant General Townshend continued to be a source of concern to the enemy's forces and occupied Penamacor and Monsanto. The bulk of the Portuguese Army advanced on Mação.

Colonel Hamilton, who continued to pursue Colonel O'Reylli's retreating forces, arrived at Escalos de Cima, where he:

> [A]ttacked 200 Spanish horses with 100 horses from his regiment (the Royal Volunteers) and from the Dragoons of Chaves. These people did wonders, the shock was vigorous, 40 Spaniards were left on the ground [and] the immense ardour [of the fight] led Hamilton's squadrons to an ambush where he lost 24 men, who were left either dead or wounded, but the event is very honourable to him and to the Portuguese Cavalry.[64]

Following this, the Count of Aranda withdrew his forces to Spain, while requesting the Anglo-Portuguese Army to treat the sick and wounded that he had left behind in Castelo Branco in a humane way. This development was apparently the result of several factors. These were the combined action of the Anglo-Portuguese forces, which had converged on the forces of the Franco-Spanish Army that still remained in Portuguese territory; the bad (cold and very rainy) weather, which had made the movements of the units difficult and had affected the troops which had been living under precarious conditions; and low morale within the Bourbon forces, which was a consequence of the failure to act and the poor living conditions of the troops. On the latter

64 Anon. 'Carta do Conde de Lippe para o Conde de Oeiras, de 19 de Setembro', p.282 [original in French].

point, the Secretary of the Count of Lippe, Miguel de Arriaga, in a letter of 31 October to his uncle, reported: 'from the 26th onwards I have handed in passports to more than 100 defectors and they would be more numerous, they say, if they were not afraid of our civilians'.[65] However, even though the Count of Aranda set on withdrawing his troops, he did not do so without first ordering the demolition of the fortifications of Salvaterra and Segura, much as he had done before in Castelo Rodrigo and Alfaiates.

Everything, from the time of year to the rigour of that wintry autumn, the logistical difficulties, and the fatigue of the troops, now suggested that the Franco-Spanish Army, having recoiled back into Spain, would remain in its quarters for the winter and would only start a new campaign the following year.

With the Anglo-Portuguese army, the commanders of the various corps, for similar reasons, pressed the Count of Lippe to, likewise, instruct the units to return to their barracks and cantonments until any resumption of operations. This is what happened, although the Marshal-General also decided to introduce some changes to his deployments, considering the welfare of the troops. It was necessary to safeguard against the possibility of the enemy carrying out any isolated actions and to take into account the fact that the following campaign would have to take place in Alentejo. Thus, it would be essential to set up appropriate garrisons in the main border forts, to move more forces to the south of the Tagus, and to ensure that the intervention of the backup forces might be made in a timely manner.

The units of Lieutenant General Townshend's force settled in several settlements of Beira Baixa and occupied the crossings of the Erges. Those of Brigadier Burgoyne, while maintaining their mission of keeping watch of the Tagus in the vicinity of the hill range of S. Mamede, settled between Nisa and Portalegre. The Marvão garrison was reinforced, given the importance of this key point to control the passageway from Valencia de Alcántara to Castelo de Vide. The Elvas garrison was reinforced with one regiment and two battalions. Alegrete, Arronches, Ouguela, and Campo Maior received garrisons or were reinforced. Some regiments that were to the north of the Tagus crossed the river and established quarters in Alentejo. The British regiments and the remaining Portuguese units stayed in the region of Sardoal.

This disposition guaranteed that the Tagus would be covered up to as far as Elvas. It relied partly on the defensive value of the river Sever, which in its stretch from Marvão to the Tagus delimited the border, the hill range of S. Mamede, which restricted movement, and the various forts that complemented the minor defensive value of the terrain between Portalegre and Olivença. Furthermore, reserve forces were made available that could be sent wherever and whenever necessary.

A major concern of the Marshal-General was that the forts and fortifications should be headed by commanders who might be able to guarantee that their defence would be conducted with determination. He wanted, at all costs, to avoid the easy surrender of the border forts, as had

65 Ernesto Augusto Pereira Sales, *O Conde de Lippe*, p.29n.

been the case on multiple occasions (sometimes without the firing of a single shot) since the enemy had begun the invasion of the Portuguese territory. In fact, this concern with these forts was not new. On 12 September, the Count had already thought it necessary to put 'Campo-Mayor, Juromenha, Arronches and Olivença in condition to resist a coup de main'.[66]

Furthermore, since the beginning of September, the Count of Lippe had been insisting with the Count of Oeiras on the idea that, given the importance of the fortress of Elvas, the appointment of its Governor should not be viewed as an 'honour"'[67] Its relevance required the appointment of an official with campaign experience who might guarantee that its defence would be conducted with determination and courage. After the exchange of several letters on the subject, he succeeded, during his meeting with the Count of Oeiras in Tancos at the end of September, to have Major General Clark appointed as governor of that fort, despite the fact that the appointment of a foreigner would hurt some susceptibilities.[68]

The forces at Alegrete were put under the command of Colonel Wrey. Colonel Vaughan, an officer who had distinguished himself in British India, was appointed Governor of Arronches. Captain Brás de Carvalho remained at his post at the fort of Ouguela, which was reinforced with 50 grenadiers from the garrison of Campo Maior. At Campo Maior, the Marquis of Prado, who was an experienced man and a loyal subject, was kept as Governor, and the garrison was reinforced with two battalions. The garrison of Marvão received a troop reinforcement, as well as Captain Brown, an Irishman from Armstrong's 83rd Foot. These concerns of the Marshal-General resulted from the possibility that the Franco-Spanish Army might try seizing some border forts in order to give themselves an advantage ahead of the following year's campaigning. Indeed, such attempts came to pass.

On 8 November, six Spanish regiments crossed the ravine of Porto de Espada, in the hill range of S. Mamede, and made a reconnaissance of the axes towards Marvão. In addition, there was information that other army forces gathered in the region of Valencia de Alcántara with the purpose of taking action to capture Campo Maior.

The operation against Campo Maior did not take place, due to lack of coordination of the attacking units. Forces from Albuquerque was to join others from Badajoz, which were already close to the town, but that did not happen when expected. When the Badajoz contingent withdrew, Colonel Vaughan, together with the Regiment of Olivença, which reinforced the fort, wished to intercept the Albuquerque force. However, this action was not successful either because, as this unit had been informed about the movement of forces of Campo Maior, it had withdrawn.

These events led the Count of Lippe, on 12 November, to determine, as a matter of precaution, that the forces should leave the winter quarters and that the units that were north of the Tagus should pass the river and gather in the

66 Anon. 'Carta do Conde de Lippe para o Conde de Oeiras, de 19 de Setembro', p.267.

67 This issue is dealt with in great detail and with a degree of criticism vis-à-vis a large part of the Portuguese nobility in Pereira Sales, *O Conde de Lippe*, pp.40-44.

68 Anon. 'Carta do Conde de Lippe para o Conde de Oeiras, de 19 de Setembro', p.273.

The Combat at Nisa. This action occurred at the end of the campaign of 1762, in the beginning of November, when the Spanish army, which was concentrated in Valencia de Alcántara and was already by then under the command of the Count of Aranda, tried to attack Marvão and Castelo de Vide (Drawing attributed to Cavaleiro Faria in *Notícias dos Sucessos da Guerra de Hespanha*... (News on the developments in the Spanish War...), belonging to the Library of the Military Academy, Lisbon, doc. 2058, p. 247).

region of Fortios, near Portalegre. In this way, he placed the centre of gravity of the army closer to where the actions of enemy would probably be carried out. This disposition also blocked the axis from Marvão to Castelo de Vide, a town which, if taken by the enemy, would grant it access to the Alentejo plain. The attempt to take Marvão was thwarted by the energetic action of Captain Brown, who ordered artillery fire on a force that was approaching the fort and calling upon the garrison to surrender, thus causing several casualties and forcing it to retreat.

Meantime, the enemy gathered three divisions in the region of Valencia de Alcántara and worked on developing the means to bring up their artillery. Burgoyne, for his part, occupied the nearby heights of Castelo de Vide and increased the protection of Marvão, whose garrison was reinforced.[69]

On 12 November, an enemy force, composed of four squadrons, attempted to take Ouguela, but the valorous action of Captain Brás de Carvalho and the small garrison of the fort frustrated this attempt. The enemy force withdrew, leaving several dead on the ground, and, by way of reward for their actions, Brás de Carvalho and the garrison officers were promoted to higher ranks.

These two failures by the Franco-Spanish forces, in Marvão and Ouguela, made it clear to them that it was no longer possible to easily take the Portuguese border forts, as had happened at the beginning of the campaign. Thus, on 15 November, the enemy army, while leaving garrisons in Alcantara,

69 Schaumbourg-Lippe, 'Memória sobre a Campanha de 1762', p.707.

The Combat in Castelo de Vide. This combat belongs to a series of clashes that occurred from 8 to 15 November between Nisa and Marvão, when the Spanish army tried to attack Marvão and Castelo de Vide. These events ended with the withdrawal of the Spanish from Alentejo and a request for suspension of conflict by the Count of Aranda, which was communicated on 22 November 1762 (Drawing attributed to Cavaleiro Faria in *Notícias dos Sucessos da Guerra de Hespanha…* (News on the developments in the Spanish War…), belonging to the Library of the Military Academy, Lisbon, doc. 2058)

Albuquerque, and Badajoz, began to withdraw in order to establish barracks in Spanish Extremadura. Deployments on the Anglo-Portuguese side still troubled the enemy forces on the move, by making some more prisoners, but the last action of the campaign was made by the Alegrete garrison against Codiceira, a frontier settlement, where prisoners were also made.

On 22 November, the Commander-in-Chief of the Franco-Spanish Army, the Count of Aranda, sent Major General Bucarelli to the headquarters of the Anglo-Portuguese army in Monforte to propose the suspension of hostilities. This was proposal was accepted and signed on 1 December. By as early as 3 November, the Plenipotentiary Ministers of the nations involved in the war had signed the preliminaries of peace at Fontainebleau. Nonetheless, the definitive peace treaty was only signed on 10 February 1763 and, through it, the forts of Chaves and Almeida were returned to Portugal along with the Colonia del Sacramento on the Río de la Plata.

7

# Conclusion

From this description of the Guerra Fantástica, it is important to highlight some aspects by way of conclusion.

On several occasions, in the wars between the great powers, Portugal has tried to remain neutral. However, because it does not have a credible military apparatus (relative to those of the major powers) to enforce this neutrality, it is frequently drawn into conflicts which it does not desire or which do not serve its interests. This was very visible during the Seven Years War with the 'Lagos Case', which was closely linked to Portugal's entry into the war.

When the political power ignores or does not pay enough attention to security problems, as was the case during several years of the reign of João V and at the beginning of the reign of José I, the military apparatus becomes almost symbolic, not serving the aims for which it exists, and hard to rebuild in case of necessity.

Portugal has often faced forces that are so much greater than its own potential, as happened after the Family Compact, that it is forced to resort to the support of its allies to defend its interests. When this coincides with the interest of its allies (it was on the basis of this interest that William Pitt advocated the assistance to Portugal in the British Parliament), they come in Portugal's support. When this does not happen, Portugal is unable to be successful militarily.

Portugal has for centuries been a landing platform for the maritime powers in its clashes with the continental powers, and a line of defence of the continental powers against the maritime powers. In the Seven Years War, Portugal was invaded by the continental powers in their struggle against the maritime powers, much like it would be later, when the Napoleonic invasions occurred.

Construction and reconstruction of military power require a committed support and a close collaboration between the political power and the command of the armed forces. In the Seven Years War, this connection existed between the Count of Oeiras and the Count of Lippe and it was this link that allowed the army to be reconstructed. The letter reproduced in Appendix I is indicative of the high regard in which the Count of Lippe was held by the Count of Oeiras. This type of connection would again emerge at the beginning of the nineteenth century, as Miguel Pereira Forjaz and

Lippe's Regiment in 1764. Lippe's Regiment was created by a Decree of 10 May 1763, as it joined two regiments set up in 1762 as a result of the splitting of the former Second Army Regiment, the old Tercio of the Trade Guild or Stock Exchange. Its first commander was Luís de Sousa Macedo, Viscount of Mesquitela, who commanded it until 1785. (Watercolour by Ribeiro Artur, Military Museum of Lisbon)

William Carr Beresford built a close contact, which allowed for the creation of a military structure which distinguished itself and honoured the country during the Peninsular War.

The armed forces are not effective without competent personnel at the various levels of the military establishment. The situation in Portugal in 1762 was very serious, which is why the country had to resort to foreign staff, much as had been the case during the Restoration period and would again take place at the time of the Napoleonic invasions.

A battle is the natural locus of encounter between two armies which aim to obtain victory. Lack of a battle is usually linked to the wish by the weakest not to be defeated. However, when the difference of potentials is significant, the strongest may impose a battle. Although the Franco-Spanish army was significantly stronger than the Anglo-Portuguese army in 1762, it must be borne in mind that the Portuguese were defending their country, that the terrain chosen by the invader rendered its manoeuvres difficult, and that the Anglo-Portuguese Army had a commander, the Count of Lippe, who was a very competent and skilful chief. These factors significantly increased the combat potential of the Anglo-Portuguese Army, thus preventing the invader from trying to reach a solution through battle.

It is difficult to understand the strategic planning that sustained the invasion of Portugal in 1762, because neither was the aim of the Franco-Spanish Army clear, nor did their choice of the areas of operations seemed correct. However, these facts were skilfully taken advantage of by the Count of Lippe and the Anglo-Portuguese army. In strategy and tactics, it is important to exploit one's opponent's mistakes.

The Portuguese people have a sense of independence, which is an element of strategic potential of high value, especially when national territory is under threat. In the Guerra Fantástica, this was well demonstrated in the resistance of the militias in Trás-os-Montes, in the attempt to reoccupy Alfaiates, and, more generally, in the hostility of the population against the invader. There is a spirit of resistance that leads the Portuguese to sacrifice and to generously

Wilhelmstein. In this fortress, which started being built in 1761, the Count of Lippe created an artillery school in 1765 and a military academy in 1770. This academy became famous for having had as its student Gerhard Scharnhorst (1755-1813), the reformer of the Prussian Army after the 'catastrophe' of 1806.

shed their blood when the country is in danger. However, when threats to Portugal are not very obvious, the political power usually neglects security and defence problems, leaving the population unaware of these issues and without any motivation to make the required sacrifices.

The Portuguese soldier, characterised by rusticity, flexibility, generosity, and the capacity to improvise, is a precious asset for military institutions to be able to fulfil the missions that are assigned to them. Much like in other cases, this was proven in this conflict, as noted by the way in which the Count of Lippe praised the men in his ranks.

It is noteworthy that, 30 years after the defence of the country was re-evaluated and the army was reorganised under the enlightened direction of the Count of Lippe with the support of the Government, when it was decided that forces should be sent to the Roussillon, the military institution was, once again, unable to respond effectively to the requirements of national politics. With so many similar examples throughout the 1,000 year-long history of Portugal, it is strange that the political power in Portugal has not learnt that, when it ignores or stops being attentive to the military, it ceases to exist and to be available in case of need. This, of its own, is fantastical.

## Appendix I

# Letter from the Count of Oeiras to his son, September 1762

I have received information, by different ways, that murmurings have begun in this Army against this brilliant Marshal-General, on the basis of the argument that, in engaging in military actions, he prefers foreigners to our Portuguese nationals. I have shown, through repeated and authentic evidence, that no one can exceed me in love for the country and in the desire that my patricians exalt themselves about heroic actions. However, we must do justice to all and not let self-love drag us along until we are led down the ultimate precipice.

The Marshal-General is very skilled in his profession. He has a wide and well-nurtured experience of war. He is a foreigner in this country; he cannot yet know its nationals through their actions. He found abandoned provinces, and saw five forts surrender without the firing of a gunshot, our defence ending up limited to that made by civilians with no support from the regular troops, always placed far away from the enemies. All this put together could not but naturally very much lower down the general perception of such a foreigner about our nation. And until he knows the many worthy details which, time will be revealing to him while he is among us, it is only natural that he will always proceed with great fear, until he has acquired the experience that will show him how the current Portuguese are, who have inherited the spirits of our ancestors.

Upon going through this fair reflection about the true state of things, I find, on the one hand, that justice must be done to the Marshal, who, in such a critical conjuncture, entrusts, first of all, those he knows, rather than those who are unknown to him. I consider, on the other hand, that all our compatriots who distinguish themselves will, with great reservations, be employed by him; because he only wants to have many who may help him in the defence of this kingdom, and in the exaltation of its own glory.

This is the pure truth that you must always keep in memory, not only to avoid, but also to convince, where necessary, the ill-considered murmurings that I spoke of above, which, upon reaching the ears of the Marshal, will only serve to lower us down even more in his perception, and to antagonise him, making him lose the hope, which I know he has, of training skilled officers among our Portuguese people.

I have felt compelled by my love, and common interest with all that concerns You, to confide in you this very secret warning, which is born from the heart. With which I am always anxious to have news from You, as a father who cordially loves You.

Sebastião José

## Appendix II

# Anglo-Portuguese Army Order of Battle

Commander in Chief: Marshal-General Count of Lippe
Lieutenant Generals
- Lord Loudoun (commanding the British contingent)
- Dom João de Lencastre (General of Infantry)
- Marquis of Tancos (General of Cavalry)
- Count of Cunha (General of Artillery)
- Prince of Mecklenburg
- Dom Luis de Portugal

Major Generals
- Manuel de Bessa Dantas
- Dom Vasco da Câmara
- Marquis of Angeja
- Dom José Joaquim de Miranda
- Dom José Félix da Cunha
- Count of Santiago
- José Leite de Sousa
- Count of Soure

Quartermaster General: Major General Hon. John Craufurd
Adjutant General: Colonel Bohm

### First Line

Cavalry
- Mecklenburg Cavalry under the Prince of Mecklenburg
- Cais Cavalry under Count of Sampaio
- Alcantara Cavalry under Dom Fernando José Lobo da Silveira
- Moura Cavalry under Dom José da Costa
- Burgoyne's 16th Light Dragoons under Lt. Col. Somerville

Portuguese Infantry
- Regiment of Cascais under Marquis do Lavradio
- 1st Regiment of Lisboa under Count de Prado

1st Regiment of Corte under Count of Aveiras
1st Regiment of Setúbal under Dom Francisco Assis da Cunha
1st Regiment of Olivença under Martim Lopo Saldanha
Battalion of Grenadiers under Colonel Lee
1st Regiment of Moura under Dom António Veríssimo
1st Regiment of Castelo de Vide under Dom Fernando de Almeida
1st Regiment of Lagos under Count of Vimeiro
1st Regiment of Faro under Dom Gastão da Câmara
2nd Regiment of the Armada under Viscount de Mesquitela

British Infantry
Light Infantry Battalion under Lt. Col. William Dalyrmple
Grenadier Battalion under Lt. Col. Viscount Pulteney
Howard's 3rd Foot (Buffs) under Lt. Col. John Biddulph
Frederick's 75th Foot under Col. Corbett Parry

**Second Line**

Cavalry
Olivença Dragoons under Dom José da Câmara
Évora Dragoons under Dom Francisco da Silva Tello
Penamacor Dragoons under Henrique Garcês Palha
Bragança Cavalry under José António Freire de Andrade

Portuguese Infantry
2nd Regiment of Cascais under Dinis de Mello
2nd Regiment of Lisboa under Count of Ponte
2nd Regiment of Corte under Count of Vila Flor
2nd Regiment of Setúbal under António de Vasconcelos
2nd Regiment of Olivença under Correia de Lacerda
2nd Regiment of Moura under Diogo Monney
2nd Regiment of Castelo de Vide under Robert Wrey
2nd Regiment of Lagos under Diogo Anderson
2nd Regiment of Faro under Francisco de Lima

British Infantry
Lambert's 67th Foot under Col. Thomas Shirley
Armstrong's 83rd Foot under Col. Bigoe Armstrong
Craufurd's 85th Foot (Royal Volunteers) under Lt. Col. James Douglas
Blayney's 91st Foot under Col. Henry St John

**Artillery**

Artillery Regiment of Estremoz under Col. Valleré
British Royal Artillery (8 Coys.) under Col. Pattison

### Corps in Beira under Lieutenant General Townsend

Cavalry
- Almeida Cavalry under Dom Francisco Inocêncio de Sousa Coutinho
- Chaves Dragoons under Dom Pedro Manuel de Vilhena

Infantry
- 1st Regiment of Peniche under Brigadier Lourenço de Melo
- 2nd Regiment of Peniche under Dom Miguel de Almeida
- 2nd Regiment of Chaves under João António de Sá Pereira
- 2nd Regiment of Porto under Jorge Francisco Machado de Sousa
- 2nd Regiment of Valença under António Vieira Guedes
- 1st Regiment of Penamacor under Luís de Vasconcelos
- 2nd Regiment of Penamacor under Chevalier de Foulis
- 1st Regiment of Viana under Luís Pinto Roby
- 1st Regiment of Campo Maior under Manuel Pereira de Matos
- 2nd Regiment of Viana under Sebastião Pinto Roby
- 2nd Regiment of Campo Maior under Pascoal Pepper
- 1st Regiment of Olivença under Furtado de Mendonça
- 2nd Regiment of Olivença under Col. Lee
- Voluntários Reais (infantry and cavalry) under John Hamilton

### Corps in Trás os Montes under Lieutenant General Carey

Infantry
- 1st Regiment of Valença under Dom João de Sousa
- 1st Regiment of Bragança under Francisco Luís Pequeno
- 2nd Regiment of Bragança under Dom Luís de Sousa
- 1st Regiment of Porto under Dom António de Lencastre
- 1st Regiment of Chaves under F. B. Morais Pimentel

Cavalry
- Companhias de Éguas

# Bibliography


Anon. 'Carta do Conde de Lippe para o Conde de Oeiras, de 19 de Setembro', *Boletim do Arquivo Histórico Militar*, 1934, pp.243-284.

Anon., *Historia de España* (Barcelona: Instituto Gallach de Librería y Ediciones, 1943).

Barrento, António, *Reflexões sobre Temas Militares* (Lisboa: Instituto de Altos Estudos Militares, 2000).

Cardoso, José Marques, *Elementos da Arte da Guerra* (Lisboa: Offic. Patr. De Francisco Luiz Ameno, 1785).

Chevalier, J. Jacques, *Les Grandes Oeuvres Politiques de Machiavel à Nos Jours* (Paris: Colin, 1970).

Corvisier, André, *História Universal - O Mundo Moderno* (Lisboa: Círculo dos Leitores, 1977).

Costa, A. J. P. da (ed.), *Os Generais do Exército Português* (Lisboa: Biblioteca do Exército, 2005).

Latino Coelho, J.M., *História Política e Militar de Portugal* (Lisboa: Imprensa Nacional, 1874).

Locke, John, *Second Treatise of Government* (Indianapolis: Hackett Publishing Company, 1980).

Lúcio de Azevedo, J., *O Marquez de Pombal e a sua Época* (Lisboa: Clássica Editora, 1909).

Luz Soriano, S.J., *História do Reinado de El-Rei D. José* (Lisboa: Tipografia Nacional, 1867).

Ferreira Martins, Gen., *História do Exército Português* (Lisboa: Inquérito, 1945).

Mourinho, António Maria, *Guerra do Mirandum*, (Bragança: Tip. Académica, 1966).

Mourinho, António Maria, 'Invasão de Trás-os-Montes e das Beiras na Guerra dos Sete Anos pelos Exércitos Bourbónicos, em 1762, através da Correspondência Oficial dos Comandantes-Chefes Marquês de Sarriá e Conde de Aranda...' (paper presented at the Academy of History on 22 April 1983), *Anais da Academia Portuguesa*, II Série. Volume 31, 1986.

Palmeirim, Gen. Augusto Xavier, *Alguns Factos Militares Portuguezes do Século XVIII* (Lisboa: Tipografia Universal, 1873).

Pereira Sales, Ernesto Augusto, *O Conde de Lippe em Portugal* (Vila Nova de Famalicão: Grandes ateliers gráficos "Minerva", de G. Pinto de Sousa & Irmão, 1936).

Pessoa, Frenando, *Poesias de Álvaro de Campos, Obras Completas de Frenando Pessoa* (Lisboa: Ática, 1980).

Schaumbourg-Lippe, Conde de, 'Memória sobre a Campanha de 1762', *Revista Militar*, 1849, pp.182-187, 427-434, 536-545, 701-710.

Selvagem, Carlos, *Portugal Militar. Compêndio de História Militar e Naval de Portugal. Desde as Origens do Estado Portucalense até ao Fim da Dinastia de Bragança* (Lisboa: Imprensa Nacional, 1931).